TWO SISTERS

NGARTA AND JUKUNA

To the families of the two sisters

TWO SISTERS

NGARTA AND JUKUNA

A TRUE STORY

**NGARTA JINNY BENT,
JUKUNA MONA CHUGUNA,
PAT LOWE, EIRLYS RICHARDS**

Magabala
Books

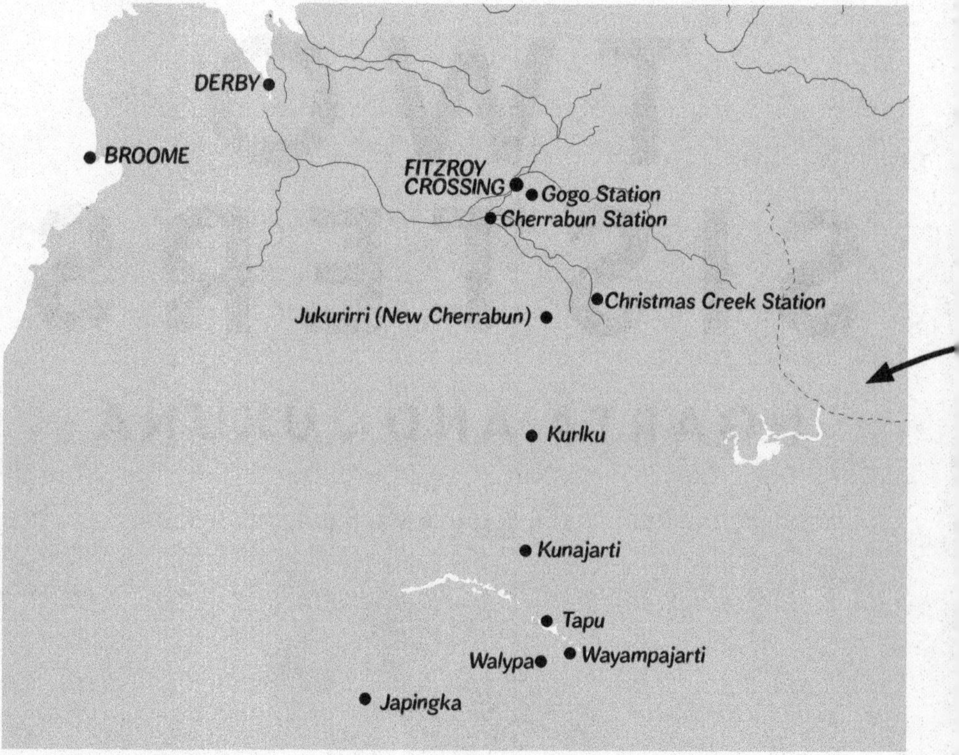

DERBY

BROOME

FITZROY CROSSING • Gogo Station
• Cherrabun Station

Christmas Creek Station

Jukurirri (New Cherrabun) •

Kurlku

Kunajarti

Tapu
Walypa • • Wayampajarti

Japingka

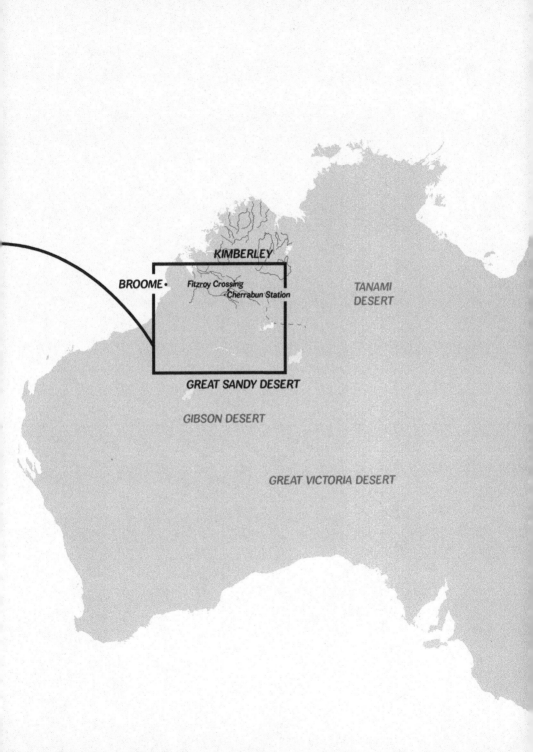

KIMBERLEY

BROOME•

Fitzroy Crossing
Cherrabun Station

TANAMI
DESERT

GREAT SANDY DESERT

GIBSON DESERT

GREAT VICTORIA DESERT

CONTENTS

N o one knows how many people were living in the Great Sandy Desert before European settlement of Australia. The desert people belonged to several distinct language groups and for most of the year they were widely dispersed over the vast country. In the late dry season, which was the main ceremony time, people gathered in large numbers at major waterholes.

When early European settlement was taking place on the fringes of the continent, the desert people were untouched. Only when the cattle and sheep stations were established to the north of their country did rumours of change reach them. The people who lived along the rivers and in the ranges bore the brunt of the European push, because their lands provided just the sort of pasture the settlers needed for their stock.

Jukuna and Ngarta are two sisters who belong to the Walmajarri/ Juwaliny language group. Walmajarri country stretches almost as far as the Fitzroy River to the north, but the family of these two sisters came from much further south, from the Great Sandy Desert proper, so that when the first Walmajarri people, the northern groups, were going to work on cattle stations, the southern groups were unaffected. However, even the bands most distant from one another were linked by marriage and consanguinity, and information about upheavals caused by the settlers of the cattle and sheep stations filtered back along the attenuated communication lines to reach even the remotest parts of the desert.

Much later, the people from further south in the Great Sandy Desert were gradually drawn into the vacuum created to their north.

The First World War came and went, and left no impression in the sandhills. Two decades later, the Second World War had faint reverberations. News reached the desert that the white people were fighting an enemy from overseas, and formations of aircraft appeared in the sky. These were probably on training exercises from air bases such as the one at Noonkanbah in the Kimberley. No one in the desert had heard of Adolf Hitler.

None of the desert people knew about the Royal Visit of the young Queen Elizabeth in 1953, or would have had any idea of what it was all about. The Melbourne Olympics three years later caused not a ripple in the lives of Ngarta, Jukuna and their family. Robert Menzies, of whom they knew nothing, was Prime Minister when Jukuna and later Ngarta emerged from the Great Sandy Desert. It would be much later before they first heard the word 'Australia' and learned that they were not only Walmajarri, but also Australians.

PAT LOWE

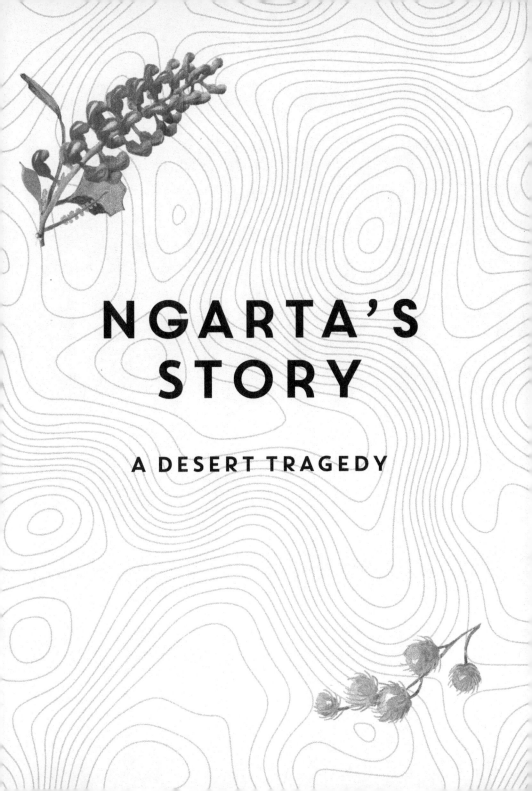

NGARTA'S STORY

A DESERT TRAGEDY

PROLOGUE

*When all but the last handful of Walmajarri people had left the desert,
two Manyjilyjarra brothers came into their country from the east.
These men were from a family of outlaws, men who lived apart from
other people and defied the law, who preyed on their fellows, killing
without reason, abducting women and discarding them. Other men
feared them, and for a long time they got away with their crimes.*

*Originally there were four brothers. Tirinja was the eldest. The
others were Yungangi, Nyuljurra and Yawa. The first three brothers
travelled together and were responsible for the deaths of a number
of people. Eventually Nyuljurra was killed in a vengeance fight
somewhere near Balgo.*

*Tirinja and Yungangi then travelled together for a time, until they
were pursued by the relatives of a man they had killed. These men
caught up with Yungangi and killed him. His elder brother Tirinja
escaped by climbing a hill where no one could reach him, and later got
away and went to find his youngest brother, Yawa. Some people say*

that Yawa was a good man, different from the other three, but under Tirinja's influence he took part in the same violent and murderous activities.

Tirinja had a son and a daughter in his group. Once, when he was displeased with the boy, Tirinja and his brother lifted him by his hands and feet and held him spread-eagled over the fire, face down, to punish him. The burn scars marked his forehead and chest for the rest of his life.

Every now and then, news of yet another killing reached the scattered bands. No one had the power to control the killers or bring them to punishment. They moved, uninvited, into country that was not their own, and eventually they went into Walmajarri country.

One old Walmajarri man and his two wives were staying at a waterhole. They were related to the people of Japingka, in whose country they were living, and they kept in touch with these relatives, meeting them from time to time at one waterhole or another. A family from Japingka was camping some way to the north, and every morning when they looked towards the south they would see the smoke from fires lit by this trio and know that all was well with them.

One day, no smoke appeared above the horizon, and the people wondered what was wrong. Perhaps the old man and his wives had moved to another place. Even so, in a single day they could not possibly have travelled so far that their fires would not be visible. The following day, again there was no early morning smoke. The people were puzzled and uneasy.

A little boy named Kurnti was playing in the sandhills not far from his mother's camp when he saw something that struck terror into his young heart. A woman was approaching across the flat, and though there was something about her that seemed familiar, that was not possible, for she was all white. Worse, she was making a terrible wailing sound. The boy turned and ran down screaming to his mother's camp.

'There's a Mamu! There's a Mamu coming up!' he yelled, breathless. 'It's all white!' A Mamu was a spirit much feared by the people of the sandhills.

The boy's mother climbed the sandhill to have a look for herself, and at once recognised the old man's elder wife, and saw that she had covered her face and body with clay mud from the waterhole, which had dried to a whitish colour on her skin. This told Kurnti's mother that the woman was in mourning. She was travelling on her own – it was clear that something dreadful had happened to her husband and his other wife.

When the woman reached the camp, she wailed in anguish and struck herself on the head until someone restrained her. Then she told the family what had taken place. A few days before, Tirinja had appeared suddenly at the camp, brandishing his weapons. Before the family had time to collect itself, he had driven a spear into her husband's side. The stranger had then seized hold of the man's young wife, and forced her to go away with him. The older woman was left behind with her wounded husband.

The old man was not dead, but the spear had gone right through his body, and he lay on the sand helpless and in great pain. In vain his wife tried to pull out the spear, but it was firmly lodged and she had not enough strength to shift it. Her efforts did nothing but increase the old man's distress. She could only stay and suffer with her husband until he died. Shocked and grieving, the woman struck herself on the head with a rock until her own blood ran. Then she took mud from the waterhole and smeared it over her face and body in the custom of a woman newly widowed, and set off alone to the north, in search of her kinsfolk.

When Kurnti's people heard this news, they cried and grieved with the old woman. Then they decided it was time to leave that part of the country. With the murderers so close, they could no longer feel secure.

This was a time of great change amongst the peoples of the desert. Most of their number had already left the sandhills. Some had chosen to migrate north or west to join relatives on the cattle and sheep stations that had become established in the more generously watered country of their neighbours. Others had been rounded up by white people and brought into the settlements. By the time the two strangers from the east started their marauding in Walmajarri country, only a few scattered groups of people remained. Desert society had so disintegrated that its normal laws and sanctions could no longer be enforced, and these men were able to intrude with impunity into other people's country and to prey on the few remaining unprotected inhabitants.

Kurnti's people had for a long time talked about moving away from their homelands and following everyone else to the stations. They must have known that in the end they would have no choice. Already they occupied country left vacant by people who had gone before them. Until this tragedy happened, they had held back from making the final move, postponing a change they had not sought and that they feared might be forever. Now, they could delay no longer.

The group started to head north towards the stations, putting distance between themselves and the murderers. On the way they met other small bands of relatives, among them Ngarta's family. They told these others the news of the murder and abduction, and advised them to follow. Some took heed, but others still held back. Even amongst Kurnti's group not everyone went ahead at once. Kurnti's brother-in-law and sisters, who already knew station life, went first, and Kurnti went with them. But his two mothers and some of the other older people, their fears abated somewhat now that the killers had been left far behind, decided to wait until the advance party returned for them.

Over the next few years, more members of Ngarta's family went north. Her uncle Kurnti came back and then left again, taking his mothers with him. Then her sister Jukuna left with her young husband. Ngarta stayed behind with a small group of women and children, waiting for the others to come back and pick them up. They waited for a long time.

Ngarta was born during the hottest time of year, before the rain, near a waterhole called Walypa, a word that means wind. Walypa is close to Wayampajarti, one of the major waterholes in that part of Walmajarri country. Her mother first knew she was pregnant one day when she had been gathering a big pile of grass seed, called puturu. Puturu therefore became Ngarta's conception totem.

Ngarta's earliest memories were of constant travel from waterhole to waterhole. Her parents walked, but she couldn't keep up for long. 'My mother or father used to carry me. Or my eldest sister, when my mother was carrying a coolamon of water on her head. My mother and father were quiet people; they didn't have arguments. It was my father who gave me my name.'

Ngarta's father had a younger wife as well as Ngarta's own mother, and she called both of the women ngamaji – mother. The younger wife was blind. Ngarta's own mother had two daughters older than Ngarta. The eldest got married when Ngarta was very young, and left the desert with her husband to live on Cherrabun Station, where he worked. The second daughter was Jukuna. While Ngarta was still quite small, her first brother was born. Her second mother gave birth to the last child in the family not long afterwards, another little boy.

The main waterhole for Ngarta's family was Tapu. The people might spend most of the year travelling through their country, camping by one or other of the many waterholes, but Tapu was the place they always came back to. Usually they came back in the hot, dry weather, and camped there until the rains started, for Tapu was a jila – 'living water' – water that never dries up. Even at the driest time of year, even in years when no rain fell, Tapu always held water.

When no one had visited Tapu for many months, the waterhole filled up with silt and became overgrown with grass and young shrubs. It looked the way any desert waterhole looks before people clean it out. But when all the silt and sand and debris had been dug out, Tapu could not be mistaken for anywhere else. The walls of the jila are of rock, almost perfectly round, and they go straight down, forming a natural well. The base of the well is smooth rock, but with two holes in it, like eyes. It is from these eyes that water seeps to fill the freshly dug jila.

Wayampajarti, the other major jila in Ngarta's country, was a double waterhole further to the south, a place with important songs and ceremonies which people still perform.

Ngarta loved her eldest sister, but she did not always get on with her second sister, Jukuna. She thought Jukuna was jealous of her, and the two girls often used to fight. Ngarta, the younger, always came off worse, and she used to run for comfort to her grandmother.

From the time Ngarta was a baby, her grandmother took care of her. Jukuna, only a few years older, stayed with their mother. Even when Ngarta got older she often went hunting and gathering with the old woman. She was closer to her grandmother than to anyone else, and liked having her to herself.

Ngarta remembered a time when the whole family was moving to a different waterhole, and she was walking along with her grandmother. On the journey the family broke up into ones and twos, so that they could hunt on the way and collect various sorts of food. They all travelled at their own pace. Ngarta and her grandmother went a different way from the others, and came quite close to Japingka.

'I don't want to go to that new place with everyone else,' Ngarta told her grandmother. 'Let us two go to Japingka!'

Japingka was a waterhole, a jila, bigger than Tapu. Ngarta's young uncles, Kurnti and Nyija, belonged to that place. It was their family's main waterhole, just as Tapu was the main one for Ngarta's family. The two families were closely related, and they often visited one another's country. If, in the hottest weather, Ngarta's parents did not stay at Tapu, they were likely to be found at Japingka. It was an important place for making rain, where big law meetings and ceremonies were held. When the word went out, hundreds of people would gather at Japingka to put boys through law and to settle disputes and inflict punishments.

This was not ceremony time, however, so grandmother and granddaughter went off by themselves to camp at the jila.

When a lot of people were gathered at Japingka for a big meeting, the men used to dig out a wide, deep hole for water, so there would be plenty for everyone to drink. But this time no one else was there, so the woman and the girl just dug a small well for the two of them. They stayed there on their own for two nights, then moved to another waterhole before catching up again with Ngarta's mother and father.

It was not unusual for people to break away from the main group for a time. They might follow tracks for a long distance out of their way, or take a detour to gather a particular food and then head for whichever waterhole happened to be closest at day's end. They kept in touch with the others and let them know where they were by lighting big grass fires. Seeing the smoke, the people in the main party would say, 'Oh, that's where they've got to. They'll catch up with us tomorrow,' and no one would worry.

This time spent travelling alone with her grandmother was a time Ngarta never forgot. The two of them hunted animals and gathered food as they went. At night they made a fire and slept beside it close to one another.

ঙ

When Ngarta was still quite small, her youngest brother, the son of her blind mother, died. He was just a little toddler. At the time no one knew quite what had happened. He had been playing in the sandhills with his uncles, Kurnti and Nyija, who were some years older than he was, when he came back to camp crying and distressed. He wouldn't eat, and he seemed to be having difficulty breathing. His mother, being blind, couldn't see what was wrong. Kurnti said later that he and his brother were eating marnta – gum from the turtujarti tree – and gave some to their little nephew. Perhaps it had got lodged in his throat and was choking him.

The little boy cried all night, and his mother was unable to comfort or help him. Early the next morning he stopped crying; he was dead.

The dead child's mother was distraught. She picked up a rock and struck herself again and again on the head, until blood was pouring down her face. Ngarta, too young to understand fully what had happened, had gone off early with her friend and cousin Kayinta to climb a tree. The two girls didn't see the stricken woman injuring herself. Only Kayinta's mother was with her at the time, and she was sick, too weak to intervene. So no one was there who could prevent the bereaved mother from hurting herself.

Later that day, when everyone was together, the family started to move away from that sad place and on to the next waterhole. But on the way Ngarta's blind mother became weak and ill. She couldn't stop grieving for the little boy who had died. When the travellers stopped to rest she sat down apart from the others and refused to eat. When it was time to go on, she wouldn't get up. 'No,' she said, 'I don't want to come with you. I can't go on. Leave me here. Just leave me and go.'

This was the sort of thing old people might say when they knew the time had come for them to die. Weary of life, unable to keep up and unwilling to burden the younger people, they would tell the others to leave them behind. Eventually their relatives would lead them somewhere away from the waterhole and leave them there alone with a coolamon of water, knowing they would not see them again.

But Ngarta's second mother was still young. Her husband was shocked when she talked about staying behind, and he wouldn't hear of it.

'No,' he said, 'I can't leave you. If you are too weak to walk, I'll carry you.' He handed his spears to his older wife and lifted the blind one onto his back. He carried her like that all the way to the next camping place.

But his younger wife did not get over her grief for her son. No one could console her. She would not eat and she hardly spoke. She sat alone under a tree, her sightless eyes staring straight ahead.

This time, when the family was preparing to move on again, she refused to go. 'She told her husband, "You must leave me here now." Her husband wanted to carry her, but she said no. She wanted him to leave her. So they took her and left her under a tree. My own mother put water for her, and they left her.'

The next day, when everyone was getting ready to set off again, Ngarta noticed that her second mother was missing. Her own mother was very quiet and looked as if she had been crying. It was clear that something was wrong.

'Where's my blind mother?' asked Ngarta. Her own mother didn't answer. But Ngarta kept asking, and in the end the older woman told her what had happened.

'She is sick. She didn't want to come with us.'

Ngarta knew what that meant – her blind mother had chosen to stay behind to die. Ngarta's father and mother had finally given in to the blind woman's wishes. During the night, while the children were asleep, they had led her away from the camping place and settled her under a tree on her own. They put a coolamon of water beside her and left her. In a few days, when the water ran out, she would die.

Now Ngarta started to cry. 'Why did you leave her?' she said. 'I don't want to leave my blind mother!' But her mother told her to be quiet. It was as the younger woman had wished, and there was nothing to be done. Sorrowfully, they went on to the next waterhole.

At their next camping place they found their relatives from Japingka. Kurnti and Nyija were there with their father and mother and their father's second wife, Paji. Ngarta's father and mother told them what had happened to the blind woman and her son. Everyone was crying.

ᔂ

About a year after Ngarta lost her second mother, her father died. The whole family was on the way to a waterhole called Kayalajarti – Ngarta, her mother and father, her two sisters and her young brother. On the journey, their father became sick.

It was a hot day and the man was feeling weak; after a time he had to stop and rest. His wife told Ngarta to stay and look after her father while she went on to the next waterhole to fetch water. She set off with her two elder daughters, leaving Ngarta and her brother with their father in the shade of a tree.

When their father seemed to be asleep, Ngarta and her brother left him lying there and went to sit under a neighbouring tree to wait for their mother's return. Suddenly, Ngarta heard her father call out, and she hurried over to him.

'He called out, "Come and sit with me. I'm finished."' Ngarta sat down beside him, but when she spoke to her father again he didn't answer. 'Only those few words, he said. Then he died.'

Ngarta comforted her young brother until their mother and sisters came back carrying a coolamon of water. As soon as she saw her children's faces their mother knew her husband had died. She put down the coolamon and cried aloud. Then she picked up a rock and struck herself on the head until blood ran. Her eldest daughter gently took the rock away from her to prevent her from hurting herself too badly. Everyone was crying.

Ngarta's mother left her husband's body where it lay, and took her children on to the next waterhole, called Lalka, where she knew she would find other relatives.

At Lalka, Ngarta's uncles Kurnti and Nyija were camping with their family. Besides their father and their two mothers, their married sister Tawaya was there, with her husband, his second wife, and their children. It was almost the same group of people who had met them the year before, after Ngarta's blind mother had died. Ngarta's mother broke the news to them about her husband, and everyone cried in grief for him. For a time after that, all the relatives travelled together.

As a widow, Ngarta's mother was jaminyjarti – that is, she fasted from certain kinds of meat. She could no longer eat the red meat of kangaroo or bandicoot, nor did she eat dingo or cat. She lived mainly on goannas, blue-tongue lizards and snakes, of which there were always plenty in the sandhills, as well as whatever plant foods were available.

All the relatives kept away from that part of the country where Ngarta's father had died. They would not return to the places where he had been living as long as there remained any signs to remind them of him. Not until rain had fallen in the region would all the footprints he had left be obliterated from the sandhills; after that, they could go back.

For many months the family went on much as before. Ngarta's mother moved around with Tawaya and her family; Kurnti and Nyija and their parents were usually nearby as well.

The family group was now quite large, and though they moved around the same country, they did not always travel together. After camping at one good waterhole for several days they would decide to move to another waterhole, perhaps two days' journey away. To get there they could follow different routes, particularly after the rainy weather, when all the temporary waterholes had been refilled and there was an abundance of water and wildlife.

Kurnti's mother might decide to take her two boys in one direction, stopping at a certain jumu on the way. Her husband, meanwhile, might set off in another direction with his younger wife, Paji. Tawaya and her husband would perhaps prefer to travel more directly to the new place, carrying water for the one dry camp they would have to make in between, while Ngarta's mother might take a more roundabout way. Old people like Ngarta's grandmother, who no longer had a spouse, usually travelled with their closest kin. Even so, they sometimes made independent decisions about the journey, as the old woman did the time she went with her granddaughter to Japingka.

By splitting up like this, people could take best advantage of the journey and of what the country had to offer. Each little group could hunt game and gather food in a different place. They cooked and ate some of what they caught along the way, and brought the rest to share with their relatives when they arrived at the new camping place.

There was nothing random or haphazard about these journeys. Ngarta's mother might choose the more roundabout route, not because she liked to walk further, but because she knew a good place to find jurnta bulbs at that season of the year, or where a particular fruit would be ripening. In planning her journey she would keep uppermost in her mind the places where she could expect to find water. If she knew she would have to take her family through dry country where there were no waterholes, she always carried a heavy coolamon of water on her head.

Tawaya's husband and her family, going ahead of everyone else, would dig out the jumu they called at on the way. Knowing others were coming behind them, they would leave a full drinking vessel ready for them at the waterhole, and perhaps gather extra firewood and leave that for them too. Then they kept on until they reached the next major meeting place.

If one group took a detour they hadn't planned, or simply wanted to let the others know where they had got to, they lit a fire. The smoke from the various fires kept everyone in touch with everyone else, even over wide distances.

ॐ

Tawaya's husband Nguluk had a brother who sometimes travelled with Ngarta's family. Ngarta called him 'uncle'. After Ngarta's father had been dead for nearly a year, it was this uncle who broke her mother's fast. He took some kangaroo fat and rubbed it onto the widow's lips. Then he gave her some meat from the same animal, which she ate. From then on, the widow no longer had to abstain from any kind of meat.

This same uncle of Ngarta's travelled with his own wife to the jila Japingka. He left his wife at Japingka and headed back to Tapu on his own. Tawaya's husband Nguluk went off hunting one day, and met his brother approaching Tapu. The two men stopped to greet one another and exchange news, then the brother went on to Tapu. Ngarta's mother was still in camp. As he approached, the man called out, 'I've come for you! When you were fasting for your husband, I gave you meat. Now you have to camp with me. You're my wife!' This was how he claimed Ngarta's mother. That night, he and Ngarta's mother slept in the same windbreak.

Next morning, when Ngarta saw Nguluk coming back from hunting, she went to meet him. 'Uncle's camping with my mother now,' she told him.

After the wet, Ngarta's new father went off on his own, south to Japingka to pick up his first wife. On the way back north he told her, 'We'll have to go to Tapu; I want to find my other wife.'

His first wife knew nothing of any other wife. She was furious.

When she and her husband reached Tapu she was still angry, and started a fight with Ngarta's mother. The two women fought with heavy hunting sticks, each submitting in turn to the blows of the other. The fight was bitter, and blood poured from the heads of both women. To stop them injuring one another seriously, Kurnti's second mother Paji intervened. She held back the elder wife to stop her from hitting Ngarta's mother. But then the husband of the two women joined in to defend his new wife, and he dealt his first wife a number of blows. Now Paji had to come to her defence as well, and at last managed to restrain the angry husband.

Eventually, everyone settled down. The two women got used to one another and, having given vent to their feelings. they shared the same husband amicably from then on. The three lived together for about a year.

By this time, nearly everybody had left the desert.

During these early years of Ngarta's life, people had been steadily leaving the sandhill country. As a little girl Ngarta had got to know many people besides her own close family – relatives and other people who came from different parts of the country to visit hers, then moved on. At ceremony times, crowds of visitors used to come together from near and far. Yet by the time Ngarta's mother went to live with her second husband, only a few people were left.

Nguluk had travelled north as a young man to work for the kartiya, the white people who now lived in the riverside country and ran cattle and sheep on land that once belonged to the riverside people, where kangaroos and wallabies thrived. He had left his work and walked all the way back to the sandhills to visit relatives and to claim Tawaya as his wife. He took her with him to the station, but

Nguluk never forgot his obligations to his wife's family, and after a year or two the couple came back to the desert. It was while they were visiting that Ngarta's mother became Nguluk's brother's wife.

Not long after that, Nguluk took his young family back to the cattle station, and with them went several other relatives, who were leaving the desert for the first time. Amongst them was Ngarta's young uncle, Kurnti.

All through the sandhill country people were seized by a great impulse to travel north into what was now white people's country. The more who left, the more there were who wanted to follow. Some left once, never to return. Others, like Nguluk, did come back from time to time, but not to stay.

A little while after Nguluk had left the desert, his brother decided to follow. He took his first wife with him, leaving Ngarta's mother and her children behind at Japingka. 'We'll come back for you next year,' he told them. But these were times of great change for the desert people, and he never came back. 'He went to the station with his first wife. They never came back. They left us for good.'

Instead, more of Ngarta's relatives went away until, at length, only a few people from her immediate family were still living in that whole region of desert. Almost all the men and youths had gone by now. Most of the marriageable girls had been claimed and taken away by their promised husbands. Only the old people remained, and the wives and children of the older men.

Kurnti came back with his nephew and age-mate, Minyiparnta. The youths made several journeys up and down between the desert and the station. At the end of their final visit, they prepared to travel back to the station taking some of the other people with them. Kurnti's brother Nyija and his two mothers were among those to go.

The people who came back gave a warning to Ngarta's mother

and the others who were staying behind with her. News had reached the station of the two brothers from the east, Manyjilyjarra speakers, who were travelling through the almost abandoned sandhill regions, preying on the defenceless bands of women and children that remained. The two men were cruel and dangerous and should be avoided at all costs.

This was not the first time the people had heard about these men. These were the same brothers who had speared the old man to death a few years earlier, and taken away his young wife. Nothing had been heard of the brothers for a long time, but now it was clear they had continued with their murderous raids. No one knew where they might turn up next.

'We'll come back and fetch you,' the young men promised the few who were staying behind. 'Next year, we'll come for you.'

Pijaji came back. He was betrothed to Ngarta's sister, Jukuna. He brought with him a bag of flour, and blankets, carrying them on his shoulders. At first the desert people thought the flour was intended to be eaten dry. They put some on the fire, but it burnt up and disappeared. Then Pijaji sat down and showed them how to mix the flour with water and make it into damper. Jukuna ate the damper, but Ngarta didn't like the look of it, and wouldn't try it. 'He brought that dry one too, dry bread. But I wouldn't have it. Even the flour one, I just looked at it. Jukuna tried it. He gave some to me, but I didn't like it. Only my grandmother and my mother and Jukuna ate it. I didn't want to.'

Pijaji went back to the station. The next time he returned to the desert, he claimed Jukuna for his wife. This time he brought a metal billycan and some tea leaves, as well as more flour and blankets. He demonstrated how to make tea. Ngarta declined the tea, but this time she tried the damper, and found that she liked it.

Pijaji left once more, with his parents and his new young bride. Ngarta stayed behind with her mother and her grandmother. Still some of the old people could not bring themselves to leave their country, and her grandmother had injured her back falling out of a tree and was unable to make the long journey. 'We'll come back for you,' Pijaji promised. 'Next year, we'll come back.' No one knew it then, but it would be thirty years before he would see his country again.

⌇

In the whole of the Great Sandy Desert, only a handful of widely scattered groups of people still lived in their accustomed way. Everyone else had gone. In Ngarta's country there remained just one small band of eight souls: Ngarta, her mother and grandmother, her young brother, Pijaji's two sisters and his second mother and grandmother.

This small group of women, girls and a boy had the whole country to themselves. With so few people to feed, they could afford to stay around the same area for much longer than they would normally have done. They did not need to travel far with each season to find new stocks of food. Besides, they were waiting for their relatives to come back and pick them up.

For a time they waited at Kunajarti, a jila to the north of their country, with good shade trees standing on a sandhill not far from the water. They lived mainly on goannas and snakes and the many different fruits and seeds of the desert. Occasionally they killed a dingo, a fox or a cat.

'They said they would come back for us. They left us when I was a little girl; I couldn't kill anything – pussycat or goanna – I only killed lizards, and that mountain devil. Well, they never came back. We stayed a long time at Kunajarti, killing lizards, waiting for Kurrapa* to come back. He went in the cold weather, and we waited two or three years.'

Eventually, tired of hanging around the same place and perhaps despairing of their relatives ever coming back for them, the group moved from Kunajarti back to Tapu, and stayed there for a while. Then they went on to Ngijilngijil, and back to Kunajarti, staying within this restricted range while they still hoped for the others to return.

Meanwhile, Ngarta was growing up. When Jukuna left with her new husband, Ngarta was still only hunting small game, such as dragon and blue-tongue lizards. As time went on she became more skilled. She learned to track and dig goannas from their burrows, and to catch snakes using just a stick and her bare hands.

One day Ngarta tracked a fox. She went hunting in the morning with her mother, leaving her grandmother at Kunajarti. Later in the day she left her mother at dinner camp and went off on her own. She found the fresh tracks of a fox and followed them right up to the fox's den, but it heard her coming and took off through the spinifex. Ngarta followed it for a long way. 'I chased him all around the place. Hot day. I got knock-up chasing the fox. And the fox got knock-up too.' Tired and thirsty, she kept on. The fox, which had to keep moving instead of being able to lie up in its burrow during the heat of the day, was slowing down. It circled around and, when it was getting near the end of its strength, ran back and hid in its burrow. Ngarta followed the fox back to its hole and knew she had it trapped. She dug away the sand with her wooden digging stick, called a kana, until she could reach the fox. Then she hit it on the back of the neck with her kana and killed it. This was the first time she had ever killed a fox. She pulled the body out of the

* Kurrapa is a shortened form of Kurrapakuta, Pijaji's nickname.

burrow and lifted it onto her shoulders, then started heading back to camp.

By the time Ngarta was in sight of her camp, it was late in the afternoon. Her mother had got back already and was worried that Ngarta had been away so long; she had been looking and calling out for her. From the top of a sandhill she saw her daughter coming along slowly, carrying the fox. Tired out after her long chase, Ngarta climbed up the slope to the shade tree where her family had their camp. Her grandmother was there, waiting for her. 'My grandmother cried for me: first time I killed a fox.'

Another time, when the family was camping at Tapu, Ngarta killed her first cat. She was out hunting with her dog Jaya when she came across the tracks of some kittens. She looked around in the grass until she found three little kittens hiding. She bent down to pick them up. At that moment the mother cat came to the attack. She flew at Ngarta, scratching her arms, then ran up Ngarta's side onto her head, still scratching and biting. Ngarta managed to shake her off, and Jaya chased the cat into the undergrowth and caught her. There was a noisy struggle, and Ngarta finished off the cat with her hunting stick and carried it back to camp. 'I've still got the scar from where that cat scratched me.'

Ngarta's grandmother used to worry about her walking so far in the heat. 'You must be careful,' she said. 'Don't walk so far. You might get burnt by the sun, or die of thirst.' But she was always proud when she saw her granddaughter coming home from a successful hunt.

The little group lived like this happily enough for a couple of years. They didn't see anyone else in all that time and, but for the knowledge that their relatives were living on a cattle station far to the north, they might have been the last people in the world. Life went on in its age-old pattern: food gathering and hunting, drawing water, making or improvising tools, cooking, camping, firing the country, telling stories around the fire. Everything was the same, yet nothing was the same now that they were on their own.

When Pijaji had left, his second father's old dog had followed him. It was a big but skinny mongrel named Pirli. There was a story about Pirli. After Pijaji's second father had died, Ngarta and her mother and her sister Jukuna had found the dog eating the old man's remains.

'He was a man-eater, that one. He ate someone: one old man, Kurrapa's stepfather. He ate him after he died. Yes, I saw him, when we came back to Kunajarti. Kurrapa was going to Timber Creek, the station. And Kurrapa's mother, me and Jukuna gave him a start and came back from halfway. And Pali, Kurrapakuta's sister. Walking, walking, walking to Jarirri. You've seen Jarirri? Well, this side, you know? That sandhill? Well that's where he died, that old man, the right place, Kurrapa's stepfather. That was before Kurrapa went to the station.

'The dog was looking at me. I told Jukuna, "Sister, see how that dog's looking at us. What's he holding? Is it meat?" We went close up, looking at him. No, my mother went quite close. "No, that's the old man he's holding." He was just looking at me, like that. As if he was ready to bite us.

'He was eating that old man who used to look after him. Eating him! My mother had come back to bury him, you know, that old man. Then she saw that the dog had eaten him, the whole lot. She could only see his head. Later on, Kurrapa came back to the same place, Jarirri. He was carrying flour, blankets. That dog was holding the old man's head. All the time he guarded it, and was eating it at the same time. Kurrapa found him. He hit himself, and he cried for his stepfather, then he walked away. That dog was sleeping there.'

Despite its grisly feed, Pijaji refused to destroy his stepfather's dog, and when he went back to the station for the second time, Pirli went with him.

One day, when Ngarta was out hunting with Pijaji's sister, Nyangarni, the two girls saw the tracks of a dog, which they recognised immediately. 'That's Pijaji's dog, Pirli!' they said. 'Pijaji must have come back! We'll have to go and see.'

In great excitement the two girls retraced the dog's tracks, expecting them to lead back to Pijaji and whoever else might have come back with him. They followed the tracks north over many sandhills, but they found no tracks of human beings. Later on, the dog found the girls and just stood looking up at them. 'It had big eyes, that dog,' Ngarta recalls. The girls realised then that Pirli had come back to his country alone.

The dog attached himself to the two girls and followed the family when they all moved camp. The people looked after Pirli and shared their game with him. After a time the dog became weak and his front legs gave way. He fell down in the spinifex. People thought he was going to die and left him behind. But some time later, after they had stopped at their next camp, Pirli turned up. This happened a number of times. The dog collapsed and they left him for dead, but he seemed to have an uncanny ability to heal himself. Each time he recovered and rejoined them.

'Maybe he was clever,'* says Ngarta. 'He was crippled and fell down, then he got up and walked away, like that, every time. Might be he sang himself, sang his two legs, and got up again. He made

* Endowed with healing power, able to 'sing' or charm himself back to health.

himself better. Well, we walked a long way, from Tapu to Walypa; crippled, still he followed us and found us.'

The whole family, with the dog coming along behind them, reached Walypa, Ngarta's birthplace, and stayed there for some time. But after a while Pirli moved on. Ngarta and Nyangarni followed his tracks for a long way south. He seemed to be heading for Japingka. 'Might be he was going back to his country. He didn't fall down halfway, he didn't die; he kept going. "All right, let him go," we said. I told Kurrapa's sister, "Leave him, he might bite us." We went back. Funny dog we had, that one.'

The two girls turned back to camp. They didn't see Pirli again.

The little group got over their disappointment that Pijaji's dog had not been accompanied by any of their relatives, and life went on much as before. They travelled around the familiar waterholes, hunting game and gathering food as they had always done. They must have started to believe that their relatives had forgotten all about them.

Then one day, everything changed.

They were camping at Jirrartu. Ngarta was standing on top of the rocky hill behind the waterhole, looking down, when she saw a man approaching. She thought it was her mother's second husband.

'Look, my father's coming!' she told her mother. Her mother came to see. 'That's not your father,' she said.

The man came closer. He was carrying spears. The two women waited, saying nothing. As the stranger drew near, he hauled off with his spear and, before Ngarta's mother had a chance to understand what was happening, he had hurled it at her. The spear pierced her through the side and sent her staggering, blood pouring from the wound.

Ngarta and her mother turned and ran. When they looked back they saw the man heading off the way he had come. Ngarta helped her mother back to the camp and told the other people what had happened. Fortunately, the spear had gone through the soft part of her mother's flesh without damaging bone or injuring any vital organ. Ngarta's grandmother put medicine on the injury and then chanted healing songs over her daughter. After a time the wound healed.

All this happened in the cold weather. The stranger didn't come back, and the women hoped he had gone far away. They realised he must be one of the two murderers they had been warned about, so they headed off in the opposite direction. They travelled to Ngijilngijil and Kupantartu – two jila not far from Kunajarti. When no one seemed to be following them, they went on as before. After the wet they walked back over the same country and stopped at a jumu near Jirrartu, called Marralkujarra. There was no sign of the stranger – no new tracks had appeared anywhere nearby – and they began to feel safe again. What they did not know was that the brothers were on their trail.

After a while, Pijaji's mother and her two daughters decided to walk to Ngijilngijil again, hunting on the way. Ngarta stayed on at Marralkujarra with her mother and grandmother. By now, her grandmother was quite elderly. Because of her bad back, she walked slowly, with the help of a stick.

One day, one of their dogs went hunting in the direction of Jirrartu. When the dog came back later in the day, someone was following her tracks.

As before, the strangers arrived without warning and, before anyone could speak, one of them hurled a spear. This time, the victim was Ngarta's much-loved grandmother.

'The two men came up, and straight away they speared my

grandmother. They killed her, no reason. I was crying for her.'

The spear pierced the old woman's ribs, and she fell to the ground, bleeding, and died where she lay. Ngarta cried bitterly for the old woman, who had meant more to her than anyone else in her world. The man who had thrown the spear, Ngarta later learned, was Yawa.

The two men were accompanied by a group of women and children. Amongst them Ngarta noticed a girl of about her own age, with light-coloured hair.

The men talked fast in a language Ngarta didn't know. 'I couldn't understand what they were saying. They were talking Manyjilyjarra, and I don't know that language. They were asking for water. My mother knew that language and she told me to give them some water. I was frightened, I didn't give them. My mother gave them water.'

The men moved in and took over Ngarta's family. They followed the women who had gone to Ngijilngijil, and caught up with them at a place called Wurnpu. Then they all moved on to Kupantartu. From that time on, everyone travelled together as one group.

Ngarta learned that the light-haired girl was the daughter of the two men. Her actual father was an older brother of theirs, who had been killed some time before. The girl's name was Jurnpija. She had a sister and two brothers, and her mother was expecting another child.

Ngarta's brother was the only boy in her group before the two men joined them. By this time he was approaching puberty. One day at Kupantartu the men sent Ngarta with her mother to fetch water. When the woman and girl came back they found their relatives sitting in heavy silence, their heads bowed. The boy was missing. At once Ngarta and her mother realised what had happened. 'The two men killed my brother. He was a big boy, like my son now. They sent me with my mother to get water. They speared my brother while we were gone, and killed him. We came back and people were sitting head down. We knew then: they killed my brother. My mother couldn't cry for her son. They told us: "If you cry, we'll kill you too." They wouldn't let her cry for her son.'

The band moved on: to Jirrartu again, then to Jarrpara. From there they went to another jumu nearby.

Ngarta lived in terror of the two men. She had seen them spear her mother and kill her grandmother and then her brother for no reason at all. She kept wondering who would be next. When she had the chance, she took her mother to one side. 'I said to my mother: "You and me'll have to go, run away in the night. They might kill us." But my mother wouldn't listen.' Perhaps Ngarta's mother was too frightened to run away, in case the men followed them. She must have wondered where else she and her daughter could go, when their only remaining relatives were here in this last little band. Ngarta made up her mind to go on her own.

The next afternoon, when the two brothers were out of sight, Ngarta ran away.

'So I went away on my own, in the afternoon. I went west. I took only a kana for hunting and a firestick. I walked on the grass all the way, till I got to Jarirri.' Instead of walking on the sand, Ngarta stepped from one tuft of spinifex to another in order to leave no footprints.

Jarirri, a big claypan, was dry, and that night she camped on a sandhill. She made a fire but saw rain approaching, so she covered the fire with grass and sand to keep it from going out. Enough rain fell in the claypan for her to get a drink.

The following morning Ngarta travelled to Tapu, where she knew there would always be water, and nearby she dug up some jurnta to eat. From Tapu she went to look at a neighbouring jumu, but it was dry. She had to camp all night without water, and travelled back to Tapu the next day.

Ngarta visited other waterholes she knew, spending time at each one, living by hunting and collecting fruits from the trees and plants and seeds from the grasses. All the time she was heading in a northerly direction. In due course she made her way to the big jumu, Kajamuka.

Ngarta had never left her desert country, but she thought she knew how to get to Christmas Creek Station. Her various relatives who had travelled back and forth between the desert and the station had described the journey to her. She had heard people talking about the direction of the waterholes they stopped at on the way, and she had a good idea of how to find them. Besides that, it was wet weather time again, and there should be enough rain falling to keep her out of trouble should she miss one of them. She made up her mind to follow her relatives and head for Christmas Creek.

There was one occasion on this journey when Ngarta failed to find water. She spent one night without drinking, but kept moving the next day. Still not finding anywhere to drink, she had to go back to the waterhole she had left. This meant spending a second night without water on the return journey.

She had almost reached her goal. She came as far as cattle station country, and within sight of the Cherrabun hills. There was nothing now to prevent her from pressing on to the station itself. But as Ngarta travelled further north, her resolve failed. For reasons she is no longer sure about, she gave up the idea of pushing on to Christmas Creek.

'I don't know why I went back,' Ngarta said many times. 'Maybe

I was thinking about my country. Maybe I was frightened for kartiya.'
Whatever the reason, she went back into the desert. 'I turned back
to Kajamuka. It was rainy time now.'

In familiar territory again, Ngarta went on with her solitary
existence. She made her way to Jirrartu.

Near Jirrartu, Ngarta came upon a single set of human footprints.
She recognised them as belonging to Pijaji's second mother, whom
she called aunty. The footprints were heading north. Ngarta
followed them. The tracks went from Jirrartu to Kajamuka, then
from Kajamuka to Parkanyungu, a waterhole at the side of a
sandhill. Ngarta didn't drink there, because she knew that the water
at Parkanyungu is a long way down, and requires a lot of digging.
From Parkanyungu Ngarta followed the footprints further north
again, to a waterhole she hadn't visited before, called Yartitirr. Pijaji's
mother had dug for water at Yartitirr, and Ngarta drank there.

'That aunty kept going, north, Tangku side, nearly found that
waterhole. No water. Old woman went back to Yartitirr. I met her
there, wounded one.' As soon as she saw the older woman Ngarta
understood why she had come away on her own. 'The two men
had speared her right through. She had the marks on her body, two
sides.' Her aunt brought more bad news for Ngarta. 'They'd killed
my mother. I knew they would do that.'

Ngarta and her aunt started travelling together towards Christmas
Creek. They had to go slowly because of the older woman's injuries.
'She was all right in the morning, talking to me, but later on, in the
middle of the afternoon, she was getting sick. She got a big lump
in her belly, hard. I sat down all day with her. I took her to a good
camp on a jilji.' Ngarta left her companion resting in the shade and
went hunting. She killed a cat and a snake. When she came back
she cooked the game and offered some meat to her aunt. But the

older woman was getting weak and refused the food. 'I can't eat – I feel sick,' she told Ngarta. 'You can have it.'

'I never thought about giving her lizard,' said Ngarta. Another man who had been speared through the body and showed symptoms similar to those of her aunt was said to have cured himself by eating raw lizards until he vomited, bringing up much of the blood that had accumulated in his guts.

Ngarta's aunt became delirious. 'She said, "Those two are looking at us!" 'Where, where?' I said. 'There, to the east, not far, near that tree!' 'No,' I told her, 'there's no one there.'

When darkness fell, Ngarta slept beside her injured aunt. 'I stayed with her all afternoon. I made a fire for her, made her sleep. Then I went to sleep.' During the night, her aunty died. 'I never knew. I just woke up from sleep, morning time, at dawn. I tried to wake her up. Nothing. I sat down. I felt her – nothing.'

Ngarta cried. She had to leave her aunt's body lying there on the sand. She ran away in tears.

Ngarta went back to Yartitirr, and that is where the two murderers found her. She had been living on her own for one full year.

঒

Near Kajamuka the two men had noticed Ngarta's tracks and the group had followed her north, to Yartitirr. They saw her aunty's body on the sandhill.

As well as Ngarta's mother, Jurnpija's mother and two younger sisters were missing, all dead. 'I don't know what happened to Jurnpija's mother. They took her hunting to get camels for meat. They took her alive. When they came back, no wife. They killed her. That man was living with Kurrapa's sister now.'

Jurnpija's father, Tirinja, had made Nyangarni his wife.

'They used to do that. They killed another sister, the mother of Jurnpija's half-brother. I never saw that woman; they killed her before, a long way off. I knew that other one, Jurnpija's mother. I was at Tapu when they killed her. Then that man took Kurrapa's sister.'

Ngarta had been away for many months and the first impulse of the two men was to kill her, but Nyangarni, in her new role as Tirinja's wife, restrained them. Ngarta took the initiative and went up to the men. 'I've seen a lot of bullock tracks,' she told them. 'We'll have to go that way, north, and follow them.'

Ngarta had indeed found cattle tracks well to the north of Kajamuka. But it was not the cattle that interested her. 'That's how I made them go to the station.'

The men did as Ngarta wanted. Everyone started heading north on the trail of the cattle. On the way, Ngarta struck up a friendship with Jurnpija, the light-haired girl who had lost her mother at the hands of the brothers, just as Ngarta had. She taught Ngarta to speak her language, Manyjilyjarra.

Although Ngarta never talked about it later, she is said to have been taken as a wife by one of the men.

The group travelled north, following the same route Ngarta had taken. Eventually they reached cattle station country. Here were a lot of cattle tracks, which led them to a bore known as Parayipirri, where they saw a windmill for the first time.

'They looked at it, at that windmill. The two men started crying, near the water. They were looking at the windmill and tank. I don't know why they were crying. Might be they were frightened of that water.'

The people camped one night at the bore, then moved on to a station camp they later learned was called Julie Yard. No one was there, but they knew they were getting close to the station itself. At

Julie Yard the two men found a drum of tar, used for applying to spayed cows to heal their wounds. They had never seen tar before and, thinking it was a kind of food, like honey, they swallowed some of it. It burnt their throats and later they vomited.

After a night at Julie Yard, the travellers kept going towards the station. They stopped at a windmill called Ngalparla, close to the homestead. Near the bore was a mob of cattle, and without a second thought the brothers speared one of the bullocks and killed it. Then the young women built a big fire to cook the meat.

While this band of desert people was busy cutting up and cooking the bullock meat, an old man from the station came along on foot, hunting goannas. He saw the group of people at the bore, and the carcass of a bullock. Knowing these were travellers from the desert, he went back to the homestead and told the boss, Don Laidlaw. Then he passed the news on to the station people, many of whom were Ngarta's relatives. They knew that hers was the last group of people still living in the sandhill country to the south, although they hadn't heard news of them for a long time and didn't know that the men with them had murdered several members of Ngarta's family.

Unaware of the stir they had caused among the station people, the travellers went on with their business of cooking and eating the dead bullock. Sated with meat, they made a camp nearby and went to sleep.

Next morning, early, after another feed of bullock meat, Ngarta and Jurnpija went down to a creek not far from the bore. They sat in the shade near the water, watching the water run, and talking. Meanwhile, a group of station people was approaching. The two girls looked round and saw the people in the distance, heading towards them. They jumped up and ran away as fast as they could. They went east, making straight for the hill called Mijalpari, where they could hide. Their companions had already seen the crowd and taken off ahead of the girls.

Ngarta and Jurnpija followed the others. They ran and ran, all the way back to Julie Yard. There everyone stopped and drank plenty of water to cool down. Thinking they were safe now, the men went off to kill another bullock. They found one some distance from the bore. They speared it, then set to work cutting it up. They didn't know that the station people were still after them, some in motorcars, others following on foot. They knew nothing of cars and the speed at which they can travel, even on rough terrain.

Near Julie Yard runs a creek, with shade trees growing along the bank. Ngarta and Jurnpija went off again together to sit by the creek. At that time of year, water was running in it. The two girls sat talking and watching the water flow, unaware of the station people who were coming up behind them. 'We didn't take notice of the birds,' said Ngarta later, laughing at her own deafness to the warning signals given by the screaming cockatoos. Suddenly, they sensed a movement and turned round, but it was too late. People were all around them, black people and white. Amongst them was a policeman. He and some of the others grabbed the two girls, throwing their arms around them to hold them captive before they could get away.

As on the earlier occasion, the rest of the group from the desert had seen the station party coming up, and had taken off. Only Ngarta and Jurnpija were captured. The station mob yelled after the runaways, telling them to come back, trying to reassure them. The policeman put Ngarta and Jurnpija in the police car, where they sat waiting, speechless with fear. Eventually the other desert people let themselves be talked into coming back. They were all loaded into vehicles and taken to the station homestead.

People kept asking the girls questions, but Ngarta couldn't understand what they were saying. Then someone heard Ngarta talking to Jurnpija and said, 'Do you speak Walmajarri?' 'Yes,' said Ngarta, glad to hear one of the strangers speaking her own language.

The kartiya gave each of the girls an orange. They had never seen an orange before. 'Don't eat it!' whispered Jurnpija. 'It might be poison. Just hold on to it.' The other people urged the girls to eat the fruit. 'That's good food, from kartiya,' they told them. But Ngarta didn't believe them. She and Jurnpija held on to their oranges all the way to the station, then threw them away.

At the station they looked around in amazement at all the buildings and gates and fences – there were so many things they had never seen before. The policeman took their photographs. Then the kartiya locked all the children in a house in case they tried to run away again.

Trixie Long was Ngarta's aunty. She had gone to live at Christmas Creek before Ngarta was born, but she knew Ngarta's mother and the rest of her family. The kartiya sent for Trixie Long and told her to talk to the girls. She asked Ngarta about her mother and Pijaji's mother and the other people she had known. Ngarta told her everything that had happened.

All the children were kept locked up at night, but let out during the day. 'They took us to the bathroom and washed us and combed out our hair and gave us our first clothes. We kept on wearing clothes after that. They locked us up every night, and we sat outside every daytime. Dinner time they brought us fruit and told us, "This is kartiya food, children." They showed us and we learned. When we got used to it, we ate it.' When they had all settled down, the girls went to live in the station camp with Trixie Long. 'They took us to the river now, and showed us.'

The two murderers were sent to prison, but not for their worst crimes. 'They took the two men to jail then, for killing that bullock. We never told the police they killed all those people. We didn't know English.'

↜

Ngarta's closest relatives were living on Cherrabun Station. They soon heard the news that the last small band of desert people had arrived at Christmas Creek. At the first opportunity, Ngarta's sister Jukuna came to see her. She came by tractor with her husband Pijaji, his cousin-brother Munangu, and other people from Cherrabun. They reached Christmas Creek in the early morning.

After such a long time during which so much had happened, there was a lot to talk about, and many tears were shed over the people who had died. Then Jukuna introduced Ngarta to Munangu. He came from the same country as Jukuna's own husband Pijaji, but his parents had taken him to Cherrabun when he was a small boy, and Ngarta didn't know him. 'They told me Munangu was my husband. They told Munangu to come and pick me up later. They said, "After Christmas, we'll pick you up."'

The Cherrabun group went on to a church meeting in Fitzroy Crossing, but Ngarta stayed at Christmas Creek. She worked at the station homestead, washing dishes.

When Ngarta had been living at Christmas Creek Station for about a year, her relatives from Cherrabun came back to fetch her. This time there was no tractor; they came on foot. With Jukuna and Pijaji came several other people on their annual holiday journey.

Ngarta didn't tell the kartiya she was leaving to join her husband, in case they tried to stop her. She left with her relatives at night. 'The Christmas Creek river was running. They came and picked me up, without asking the kartiya.' When the kartiya found Ngarta missing, they sent a man to look for her. He knew where she had gone, but he went back and told the kartiya he had lost her tracks at the creek. 'We crossed the river and went the other side,' says Ngarta. 'I went to Cherrabun with Hughie [Munangu] mob.'

Ngarta with a coolamon of seeds, c1989

Jukuna carrying ngarlka in a makeshift grass basket, c1989

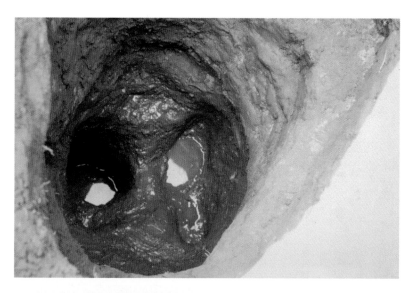

Top: Tapu, a major jila in Jukuna and Ngarta's country

Bottom: Jarrngajarti rockhole on Cherrabun Station

Right: Ngarta and Pat at Tapu, c1989

Above: Jukuna getting water from Jurnjarti jila, c1995

Right: Ngarta with her grandmother's grinding stone, c1997

Overleaf: Jilji — a sandhill

Above: Ngarta fire-raising in the desert, c1998

Overleaf: Ngarta digging Wiliyi, a jila, c1995

Top left: Japingka jila

Bottom left: Dune landscape from the air, 1988

Above: Jarirri claypan

Overleaf: Jukuna carrying a goanna after hunting
in the bush near the Fitzroy River

Top: Jukuna digging a goanna out of its burrow

EPILOGUE

It was in March 1961 when Ngarta arrived at Christmas Creek Station in the company of the two murderers and their family group. The West Australian reported that 'two primitive desert natives, Teranji and Yowunda (sic)' had been charged with killing cattle and remanded in custody for eight days. The report went on to say, 'Among the party were some children whom local natives believe to have been stolen from other tribes.' Nothing seems to have been done to follow up this allegation.

H.R. Tilbrook, District Native Welfare Officer in Derby at the time, reported that the party included two boys and five girls, ranging in age from five to fifteen. Ngarta and Jurnpija would have been the oldest of the girls. Tirinja was thought to be about 40 and Yawa 21.

The cattle killing charge against the men was reduced to 'having been in possession of beef suspected of having been stolen', for which, absurdly, Tirinja and Yawa were fined fifty pounds, in default of which they were to serve fifty days in prison.

There was a public outcry at the perceived unfairness of the sentences. The government received written protests from such bodies as the Union of Australian Women, the Joint Railway Unions Committee, the Amalgamated Engineering Union and the Federated Miscellaneous Workers' Union. As a result of the negative publicity, the men were released in April and had 'a happy reunion' with their group.

When Tirinja and Yawa were released from prison, the two men went back to Christmas Creek Station, where they were put to work. In spite of everything, Pijaji's sister Nyangarni remained married to Tirinja. She did this through custom or fear, not sentiment: 'He was cheeky [cruel] one, that one.' He was quick-tempered and used to hit Nyangarni: 'After prison, he knock[ed] me [around].'

Winingali, a niece to Ngarta, was a girl at the time all this took place, but she remembers Tirinja. She had left school and was back with her father, leading a bushman's life, travelling around the fringes of the cattle stations, tracking and hunting. One law time, she and her father were standing on top of a rise when they saw a whole army of men walking towards Christmas Creek. The men were decked out for law business: painted in red ochre, wearing ceremonial headbands and carrying spears. They were from Balgo, Winingali's father told her. They had old scores to settle with Tirinja.

As the men approached their hosts at Christmas Creek, Tirinja ran out from the waiting crowd. Shouting abuse at the visiting lawmen, he brandished his spears and yelled defiantly, 'Yes, come and get me! Come and kill me!'

The men advanced, spears at the ready, but then the Christmas Creek people intervened. They moved in and surrounded Tirinja, protecting him with their bodies. Some of the men remonstrated with the new arrivals, telling them to spare the life of the guilty man. It is hard now to understand how anyone could have agreed to spare the two murderers, but it seems that Pijaiji, whose sister was now the wife of Tirinja, interceded for his brother-in-law, as he was obliged to do, and saved Tirinja's life. Other men from Christmas Creek told the lawmen to use sorcery against the murderer: 'Don't kill him now; kill him later on, blackfella way.'

Known as Maruwajarti — the guilty one — amongst the Fitzroy Crossing people, Tirinja settled down happily enough to station life. Kartiya who remember him say he was a funny fellow, always laughing. Later, he left Christmas Creek and went to work on Leopold Station, where he eventually met his death in an extraordinary accident. It is said he was helping with work on a windmill, and had climbed onto a tank stand. The rods had been pulled up and one of them removed. He was leaning over to look down the borehole when the wind moved the sails of the mill. The exposed end of the rod came down on the back of the man's head, knocking him down and killing him instantly.

Locally, it is said the fatal accident was the result of payback, that Tirinja had been sung by the old men in revenge for the many murders he had committed.

Nyangarni was not deeply moved by her husband's death, but she observed the formalities: 'I was in Derby Hospital when they told me my husband got killed. I cried a little bit and ate fish [as required by custom], that's all. Then I went back to station and sat down [in sorry camp]. I gave out blankets at funeral. Then I went to station.'

The younger of the two guilty brothers, Yawa, disappeared from Christmas Creek Station not long after his elder brother's death, leaving behind his blanket and other belongings. People say that he had been detailed to chop wood and had failed to work hard enough to satisfy the kartiya, who 'growled' at him and struck him. Yawa waited till the kartiya had gone. Then he put down his axe, walked into the scrub to pick up the spear and woomera he had stashed away, and left the station. According to Nyangarni, who was working on Christmas Creek Station at the time: 'The other boy [Yawa] was working near the river. He left a sign – a cross on the ground – to tell people he was going back to desert, and he crossed the river. People cried for him.'

Alone and on foot Yawa headed south, back into the desert, and was never seen again. It is said he left no tracks.

〜

In 1982, maybe twelve or fourteen years after Yawa disappeared, anthropologist Kim Akerman was on a field trip with some people from Yakayaka when they stopped to check on a soak. One of the party spotted a single set of human footprints, which everyone examined excitedly. They said the tracks were only one day old, and identified them as belonging to Yawa.

The following morning, after travelling into rocky country where there were many small caves, the people found evidence of recent habitation: charcoal, half-burnt sticks, flakes of stone. This, they said, was Yawa's wet season camp. A day later, as if in verification, they found Yawa's clear footprints preserved in dried mud, prints he had made when the claypans were full of water.

Later that morning they came upon a tree from which a large piece of bark had been removed from a thick curve in the trunk, in the shape of a deep coolamon. The men went to look around, and when they came back they told Kim that Yawa had cut the bark container to carry a large number of eggs he had taken from an emu's nest to the east.

When the travellers got back to Balgo, there was some discussion as to whether a search party should be organised to find Yawa and bring him in. In the end, it was decided to leave him be. Yawa could not have failed to know that people had been around: he was on foot, never far away, and he would have seen their camp fires, heard their vehicles and seen their car tracks and their footprints. Some of the footprints would have been as familiar to Yawa as his were to the people looking for him. He could have shown himself to them at any time, but he chose to stay away.

He was not quite alone, however: wherever the man's footprints went, they were accompanied by the tracks of a dog.

NATIVES FACE CHARGES

FITZROY CROSSING, Wed: Two primitive desert natives, Teranji and Yowunda appeared in court here yesterday and were remanded for eight days on charges of illegal killing of cattle.

They were members of a party of 11 natives whom the police met while investigating illegal cattle slaughter, 20 miles from Christmas Creek.

Among the party were some children whom local natives believe to have been stolen from other tribes.

Teranji and Yowunda came into court wearing only a cloth tied round the waist, and their knotted hair hanging down on their shoulders.

They were taken outside and bathed by police trackers, who also trimmed their hair and provided them with clothing.

Article from
The West Australian,
16 March 1961

43

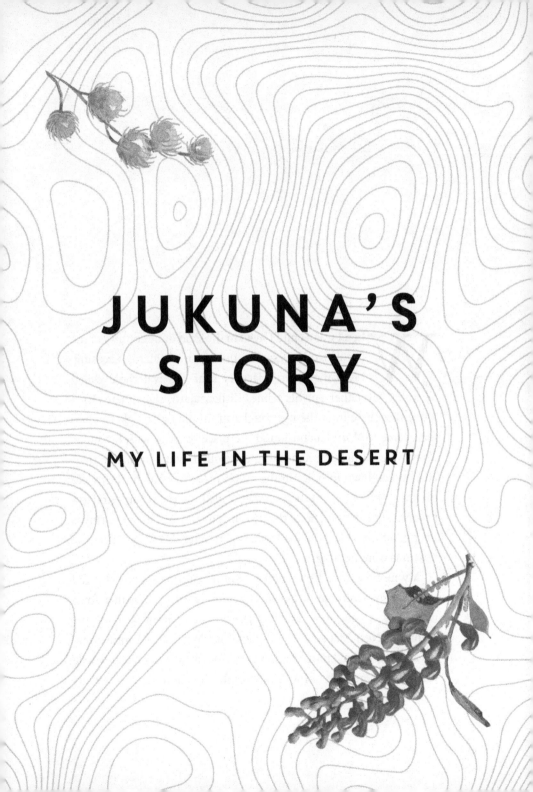

JUKUNA'S STORY

MY LIFE IN THE DESERT

JUKUNA'S

When I was a child I lived in the sand dune country of the Great Sandy Desert to the south of Fitzroy Crossing. My father's birthplace is near the waterhole called Wirtuka. My father got his name, Kirikarrajarti, right there. It's a name that came from the ngarrangkarni. In the ngarrangkarni, two men came to Wirtuka and found the place overrun with possums. They were all fighting and biting each other, some up in the trees and others down in holes in the ground. As they fought they were hissing, 'Kkir! Kkir!' so the two men called the place Kirikarrajarti, because of the hissing noise the possums made. My father's jarriny is the possum, and he is called Kirikarrajarti after this place where the possums were fighting.

My mother came from another group of people, who belonged to Japirnka waterhole. When my parents had been together for a while, I was conceived, and my jarriny comes from near the jila Mantarta. Near Mantarta is a smooth sandhill called Lantimangu. It's a place where spirit children live. When a husband and wife walk near there, one of the spirits thinks, 'I'll go to them. I'll make them a mother and father.' One time my parents got a lot of edible gum from turtujarti trees that were growing all around there, on the flat down from Lantimangu. That night my father had a dream and saw a child standing behind him, but when he turned around it disappeared. Next day he said to his wife, 'This gum might be the jarriny for our baby.' He had a feeling about it. Then my mother knew she was expecting me, and so my spirit comes from that sandhill called Lantimangu.

There was a really bad spirit child living at Lantimangu. He was my spirit brother. He threw a fighting stick at my grandmother and hit her on the back because she was digging up a root vegetable from his place. He snatched the roots from her and left her there on the ground, crippled.

My mother's father also came from the Japirnka waterhole, but his wife, my grandmother, was from Mayililiny waterhole, to the east, near the Canning Stock Route. My grandfather travelled over there and brought her back to be his wife. My father's mother belonged to Tapu and Wayampajarti, two waterholes north of Japirnka.

My mother had four children, three girls and a boy. My father had two other wives besides my mother. His second wife, who was my mother's sister, had three boys and a girl. My father's third wife had a girl and a boy. All ten of us had the same father.

Our regular journeys for hunting and collecting food took us around the country to the north and to the south of Mantarta waterhole. Although Mantarta is a jila, there is no kalpurtu living in it.

When I grew older I learnt to kill animals to eat. I killed dragon lizards, the thorny devil, the crest-tailed marsupial mouse and the dunnart. I cooked them myself and ate them. Sometimes my grandmother or older sister would kill a blue-tongue lizard or a great desert skink for me.

After the wet season, we'd leave Mantarta and hunt and gather around the freshly watered country. As we travelled we drank water from pools on the swampy ground, then we returned to Mantarta. We hunted and gathered west of Mantarta, getting water from the jumu Nyalmiwurtu, Lirrilirriwurtu, Yirrjin, Warntiripajarra and Pirnturr. These were jumu we drank from as we travelled about after the wet season.

One hot season before I was born, my father's mother, Kurnmarnu, died. She was travelling with my mother and father and my older sister. They took her to the jumu Warntiripajarra, but found that the water had dried up. They were in the middle of nowhere, a long way from water. My grandmother was too weak to travel on to the next waterhole, so they left her in the shade with a little water in a coolamon. Then they covered her up with damp sand from under the tree to keep her cool, and went on to the nearest jila, Warnti. Warnti is a long way from Warntiripajarra, and they walked all night. Other relatives were there already.

My mother filled a coolamon with water and carried it all the way back to her mother-in-law, but when she got there she found that Kurnmarnu was already dead, lying there in the shade where they had left her. She had died of heat and thirst.

In her grief, my mother hit herself on the head with a rock, making her head bleed. I think she covered her mother-in-law's head with leaves, then she came back and joined the others at Warnti. Everyone cried for my grandmother.

Our journeys also took us to quite a few jila south of Mantarta — Wirtuka, Paparta, Mukurruwurtu, Warnti and Japirnka. In the cold weather, we travelled north to other jila. We went to Walypa, then to Wayampajarti, Wirrikarrijarti, Kurralykurraly and to Wanyngurla. At Wanyngurla there were a lot of jurnta to gather and eat. We also went to Tapu, then Kurrjalpartu, Wiliyi and Kayalajarti.

Following the rainy season and right through into the cold season we gathered many different grass seeds to eat. These are the names of the grasses: nyarrjarti, puturu, ngujarna, nyalmi, manyal, jiningka, purrjaru and karlji. We call this kind of food puluru. We also gathered jurnta. Another food we gathered in that season was the nectar from various hakea and grevillea blossoms. We used to suck the nectar from the flowers or soak the flowers in water to make a sweet drink.

When the hot season came, we gathered seeds from acacia trees. We also collected flying termites that we found in antbed. People used to go looking for them in the early morning with a heavy stick, and smash the antbed to get them. They used a coolamon to separate some of the termites from the dirt and covered the rest with sand to pick up later. When they came back they uncovered them, separated them and then took them back to their camp. They put the termites out in the sun to dry and left them there until they were crisp. Only then were they ready to eat, after the sun had done its work. Everybody ate them – they were delicious.

We used to eat a desert nut called ngarlka. The nuts dropped to the ground when they were ripe. The whole year round we could gather them from under the trees, in the hot season and the cold season. We could eat them any time. The new nuts hang there on the trees unripe until the hot season comes.

For food we used to hunt and kill feral cat, bandicoot, dingo, fox, two kinds of hare-wallaby, sand goanna, different kinds of snake, rough-tailed goanna, blue-tongue lizard and echidna.

We travelled like that year after year, from one waterhole to the next, drinking at jila and drinking at jumu, at rockholes and at claypans, hunting animals and gathering the fruit and seeds of the land.

A good rainy season made the grasses grow well and gave us many kinds of seed and plenty of nectar from the flowers. In a poor wet season, very little grass grew and there wasn't much seed for us to gather. In a good year with a lot of rain we were able to store away the seed to eat later on.

To store the seed we would strip some bark from a paperbark tree to wrap the seed in a parcel, or we'd gather some strong grass and use that to make a container like a nest for holding the seed. We wrapped the seed tightly in packages, and tied them up. Then we cut four forked sticks from a tree, put rails across, and built a frame on top of them. We arranged parcels of food wrapped up in grass or bark on the frame. Then we built a small hut over the top of it to prevent the food from getting dry. We left it there so that we could come and get it later when we needed it and the trees no longer had seeds.

Sometimes we stored seeds, particularly acacia seeds, in a hole in the ground. We used to line the hole with grass, put in a layer of seeds and cover it with bark and then sand. Later, when there was no food left in the bush for us to gather, we came back to get it. We pulled the seeds out of the hole. To get rid of the strong wattle seed smell, we washed them. We cooked them in the fire and then ground them with water till they became a paste, and we ate it like that.

When people went hunting for animals in the hot season, they made sandals for themselves from the bark of the yakapiri bush. And that is what they called the sandals, yakapiri. These protected their feet from the burning hot sand. They speared foxes, feral cats, hare wallabies and sand goannas. The hare wallaby has disappeared from the desert now.

Sometimes in the hot season, we'd set off to a waterhole a long way off. We'd set off late in the afternoon, when the day was a little cooler, carrying water in our coolamons. As we walked, we drank the water until there was none left. When it was time to camp for the night, the adults found a claypan that had recently held water. They dug up some of the damp clay and threw it around on the ground to make a cool place for us to sleep. We set off again early in the morning while it was still cool, and went on to the jila.

I'll tell you some more about when I was a child. I was taught to use a coolamon for separating seed from the sand and bits of grass. My grandmother took my hands and held them under the coolamon. 'This is the way you separate the seed,' she said, as she showed me how to shake it. She taught me not to jerk the coolamon around, because then the seed wouldn't separate properly. I didn't really master that separating action till a long time later, when I was bigger. By then I could do a good job of separating the seed from the debris.

I learned to cook meat in the same way. I used to kill small animals and bring them home uncooked. My grandmother and I lit the fire, then she said, 'Bring me a yirnti and we'll cook the meat. You must leave the meat in the coals until it's well cooked. You can't eat it if it's only half done. You can only eat it if it's cooked properly.'

I also learned to cook ngarlka nuts by moving them around in the fire. When we had raked them about in the coals for a certain length of time, they'd be just right to eat.

Sometimes a mother dog brought back lizards and regurgitated them whole for her puppies. We snatched them from the pups and rolled them in the sand to clean off the slime. Then we cooked them on the fire and ate them.

My grandmother used to tell me about the people with the pink skin, called kartiya. I was curious and kept asking her about them. I imagined kartiya were like trees or dogs or something.

'What are kartiya like? Do they look like blood? Or are they like ashes? Tell me.'

She'd answer, 'No, they are like people. They have two eyes, a mouth and a nose. And two hands.'

'Do they have hair?'

'Yes, of course they have hair.'

I had often seen blood. When I killed a small lizard, some of its blood dripped onto my hand or onto the wooden shovel. 'Are kartiya the colour of this blood from the lizard?' I'd ask.

'Yes, just like that.'

I was really curious about these kartiya.

Later, when I was older, my grandmother told my sister and me to take some seed bread to the man they had arranged to be our husband. He in return sent meat to my mother. He couldn't bring it himself, because it wasn't permissible for him to deal directly with his mother-in-law.

The marriages were arranged like this: the grandmother of a small girl (on her father's side) chooses the man who will be the little girl's 'son-in-law'. The grandmother says to the man she chooses, 'This little girl is your mother-in-law. Now you have to keep bringing her meat until she grows up.' Then they give the girl a husband. When she has a baby – a boy or a girl – she promises that child to the son-in-law already chosen for her by her grandmother. If her first child is a boy, she will give him to her son-in-law first, and afterwards, when she has a girl, she will give her to him to be his wife. The boy will stay with his 'husband', who looks after him for some of the time until he grows up. When the boy is ready to go through law the 'husband' has to tie the hairstring belt around him.

When I was old enough, my young sister and I were sent to our husband, whose name was Pijaji, to live with him. My sister was still only a girl.

ॐ

Some time later our husband said to us, 'We'll go north to the cattle stations – my father and two mothers, my two grandmothers, my mother-in-law, both of you, my wives, and my sisters as well. When I travelled up there before, I saw there was plenty of food and beef belonging to the white people. I want to take all of you with me because if I leave anyone behind, strangers may come and kill you after I've gone.'

Pijaji knew about two murderers, that is why he said that. The men, from further south, had already speared a man and his mother belonging to Pijaji's family group.

My grandmother and Pijaji's grandmother and the two women he called mother said to him, 'Leave us here, we'll stay in our own country. You can't take us. Leave us here in the land where we belong. You can't take us to that station. It's too far for us to walk.' The grandmothers were getting really old, needing a walking stick to help them along. My little sister didn't want to go away and leave them. She wanted to stay behind with her mother and grandmother and her little brother.

When the winds of the cold season had finished, we got ourselves ready and set off northwards for the station country. My husband

Pijaji and I took with us Pijaji's father and mother and his young sister, Pali.

Travelling north, we went through Yarntayi, a wide stretch of flat country with few trees or sandhills, and kept heading north. We stopped and camped the night. Early in the morning we set off for the jumu Larrilarri. We didn't find any water there; it was too deep under the ground, so we kept going till we reached another jumu called Pirljiwurtu. We drew some water from there to carry in our coolamons, and drank it while we walked. The sun was low in the sky before we reached another waterhole, so we camped the night on a sandhill.

When we rose in the morning we saw that we were close to the hill called Jarrngajarti. We hadn't seen it the night before because it was dark when we stopped to sleep. We walked towards that hill and found some water in a rockhole. We saw cattle there, drinking from the pool. I had seen cattle once before: they had come all the way across to Kurrjalpartu waterhole in the desert. They must have escaped from the Canning Stock Route and travelled all that way west. Pijaji had speared one of them, and we had eaten the meat. Here at Jarrngajarti we drank from the rockhole and continued walking north past another rockhole called Jinpirimpiri.

By now we were coming close to a cattle station *bore*. We learnt later that it was called Timber Creek. It was night time, and Pijaji told us all to stay some way off, hiding in the scrub south of the bore camp. He went on ahead to talk to the man and his two wives who lived there, looking after the bore. They recognised Pijaji from his first visit to the station. The younger woman said, 'Hey, look who's here!'

The other one called out to him, 'Come over here! Come and tell us the news.'

Then Pijaji said to the man, 'I've brought someone to see you: it's my father, your son.'

'You'll have to bring him here,' said the woman. Then they gave Pijaji some damper and meat to eat.

'Yes,' Pijaji said, 'I'll bring him over later.'

The next night Pijaji took me and his mother and father and sister over to see those people. We had to go at night, because we were frightened the kartiya would see us. We all cried together.

Then Pijaji said to one of the women, 'Here are my father and mother. This is my wife.'

The woman asked him, 'Tell me, which family does your wife come from?'

'You know your sister, Nakayi, who left the desert and went north to Gogo Station a long time ago? Well this is her granddaughter.'

'Oh, I see. Then I call her granddaughter too.'

We stayed with them at the bore for a good while, maybe a month. Then one day Pijaji said to the old man, 'We'll be going now. We want to go further north to that other bore, Jukurirri. I want to find my uncle.'

'Of course. Go and look for him,' he said. So off we went.

We arrived at Jukurirri bore. My husband Pijaji told us, 'Stay here in the shade. Father, I'll go and find your brother-in-law.' Pijaji found the man, who was also his uncle, and said to him, 'I've brought your brother-in-law to see you.'

'Good. I want to see him straight away!'

Then Pijaji brought his father Maruwanti over and said, 'Here's your brother-in-law to see you.' He sat him down facing the south. They cried together because it was so long since they had seen one another. Then the man gave us some meat and damper to eat and we camped there the night. The next day my husband said to his uncle,

'I'll leave my father here with you until I get back.'

After we'd gone, the uncle, who lived at Jukurirri, said to his brother-in-law Maruwanti, 'Come with me. I've got something to show you.' They went up to the water tank on top of a rise. His brother-in-law looked over the wall of the tank and saw all the water lying there. He staggered backwards, shocked. He picked up a piece of antbed and called out to the water, 'It's me! I've come here!' Then he threw the antbed into the water, as he would have done in the desert when he was approaching a jila, to let the kalpurtu know he was coming. He didn't realise what the tank was. His stomach lurched in fear, because he'd never seen water like this, south in the desert. He was speaking to the kalpurtu he believed was in the tank. That kalpurtu lives in a jila and is in charge of the water. If a stranger comes and it can't recognise him, then a fierce wind comes up which might take the stranger's spirit and put it into the water for the kalpurtu to swallow. The brother-in-law who lived at that bore said, 'That's not a jila, it's just water they bring up with a pump from underneath the ground. Right, now we'll go back to the camp.'

Meanwhile, my husband and I walked north to another bore called Purlkartujarti where some station workers were building a water tank. It was late when we arrived and we slept the night there. In the morning one of the head workers, a half-caste fellow named Barney Lawford, saw Pijaji. He said to the working men there, 'I want that boy. I want him to come and work for me.' So they picked us up. We climbed onto the truck and they took us off north somewhere to start work. This was the first time I had even seen a truck and as we drove along I looked at the trees, which seemed to be racing past. I was frightened and crouched in the back of the truck with my head down. I'd never experienced anything like this before.

They took us north to a billabong called Warrpipakarti where men were cutting trees to make fence posts. I was given the job of helping Junyju, Pajiman's wife, with the cooking. I just watched her mixing and kneading the flour to make damper, because I didn't know how to do it.

After a while they took us back south to Jukurirri in the truck. From there we picked up Pijaji's mother and father and took them to Timber Creek outstation. That was the first bore we had stopped at, where we ate food when we came out of the desert. While we were staying there this time, my aunty, Japirirri's mother, and Pijaji's mother passed away. They died on the same day, one in the morning and the other at night. We were filled with grief and cried for them. The two widowers didn't cover themselves with mud and sit down to mourn, as people do today in the Fitzroy Crossing area. That was not our custom. When we were living around the waterholes in the desert, widows and widowers didn't put mud on their bodies.

One time at Timber Creek, one of the workers brought in some grog from the town for Christmas celebrations. The men drank it until they lost their senses. They drank the lot. As we watched them we became quite scared, because we had never seen anything like it before. We were frightened they might kill us in their drunken state.

Some time later we took the two widowed men and the two children, Pali and Japirirri, north to Cherrabun Station. When we arrived, the people there who worked on the station all stared at us, wondering who we were. We only recognised one person there, a woman who came from my country, whom I call 'mother'. When we had all identified ourselves we cried together, because we were related to one another and were meeting for the first time. We stayed there, becoming part of a very big group of station workers.

The people there sang the corroboree Julurru to welcome us. First, in the middle of the afternoon they took us with our blankets, walked us a long way west, and had us camp by the river. Next morning they took us out to the flat where they held the corroborree. They pulled hats down over our heads so that we couldn't see, and we had to keep our heads down and look at the ground, with our hands on our stomachs, because this ceremony was new to us. Then the station people all came along, singing. After a while they said, 'Look up!' Then we were allowed to look up and see the dancing. As part of the dance, they burnt each other on the back with firesticks. The dancing and singing went on all night; we didn't sleep. In the morning they gave clothes and food to one another. This was also part of the ceremony.

ᔓ

It was at Cherrabun Station that I saw a kartiya for the first time. He was the station manager, Mr Scrivener. I thought, 'So that's what a kartiya looks like!' I stared at his red skin, so different from black people's skin. He was the boss and he gave us rations in return for our work.

We worked for the manager at that station for about two years and became quite skilled at station work. I used to milk the goats, filling the bucket. Before that, I didn't know anything about milking goats. One day the manager said to one of the old women, 'Get this woman to work with you, milking the goats.'

'Okay,' she said and came and got me. 'Help me with the goats,' she said.

I thought, 'This animal looks like a dog.'

The old woman said, 'Be careful to hold its back leg, or it might kick you.' When we had milked the goats, we took the buckets of milk inside and beat up the cream to make butter for people to spread on damper or bread.

I also learned about making soap from bullock fat. We mixed up the melted fat with soda in buckets. Then we poured it into a wide shallow dish, covered it with hessian and left it to set overnight. In the morning it had hardened into soap. We cut it up into pieces and gave it to the workers for washing their clothes.

Another kind of work we did was to carry the boxes of groceries from the truck into the station store. The truck brought food and other things from town regularly.

The manager used to drive us out to where the cattle were grazing. He'd shoot a beast with his rifle and we women would cut up the meat and throw the pieces onto the back of the truck. He would then drive us to the meat house and we would rub salt onto the pieces to preserve it so that it could be eaten later.

There is one more thing we did. We women would paint the empty fuel drums laid out on the airstrip with white paint so that the pilots in the planes would see where to land. Those are the things I learned to do when I came to the station from the desert in the south.

～

At Cherrabun Station we lost many members of our family from sickness. We had never had such sickness in the desert. My father-in-law died there, and it was there that my husband nearly died, but because he received his dying father's spirit he recovered and went on living. My father-in-law gave his life to my husband. I was well, I didn't get sick, so I looked after the three children who had lost their parents: Pali, Japirirri and a young boy, Nyija.

My husband was very weak, so one of the family had to carry him on his back to another camp, away from the place where his father had died. A day later we set off for the south under cover of darkness, because we didn't want our relatives to try to stop us from going. We were heading back to our home in the desert. My husband was weak so we walked slowly. We took the two orphans, Pali and Nyija, with us, and we made our first camp at a sandhill along the way.

In the morning my husband was hungry and said to the boy, 'I'll take you hunting. You can find me a crab.' Pijaji was still feeling a bit weak.

'Okay,' Nyija said. They found a crab hole.

'Put your hand into the hole,' Pijaji told Nyija. The boy put his hand in the hole and felt around till a crab bit his hand.

'Ouch, it's bitten me and it hurts!' His hand was bleeding. Then Pijaji started pulling a whole lot of crabs from the mud. They cooked them and ate them.

Some of our relatives, a man and three women, had followed us from Cherrabun, and they arrived at the sandhill where we were camping. One of the women was sick. She was the sister of Nyija's mother, so he called her 'mother'. The next day we said to them, 'We're heading south now, are you coming with us?'

The sick woman replied, 'No, leave us here. I'm staying here.'

Nyija said, 'No we'll take you along with us, Mummy.'

'No, if I go I might get worse along the way,' she said.

The little boy cried for his mother to come with us, but she couldn't.

We kept going south, and in the late afternoon we reached Jukurirri. We sat down there in the shade and I cooked a goanna I had caught. Then my husband saw a small crow sitting on the branch of a tree. He said to Nyija, 'Kill that crow for me son.' The boy ran over to the tree. 'Climb up the tree and kill the crow,' Pijaji told him. Nyija got a stick, climbed the tree and killed the crow.

After it was cooked, they ate it between them.

While we were there, my husband said to the boy, 'Son, we're going to take you back south to the jila country. Living in this station country has made me sick.'

The boy said, 'No, I can't go to the south, it's too far for me.'

Nyija went off to tell another man who was camped at that place, whom Nyija called 'father'. He said to him, 'Father, those two are going to take me with them when they go south back to their country.'

The old man didn't say anything. The boy kept on telling him, 'Those two are going to take me to the desert with them.'

Then the old man spoke. 'No. None of you should go. You must stay here. Pijaji might get sick again along the way.'

'Okay, I'll tell him,' said the boy.

When he saw Pijaji, he said, 'My father says we mustn't go back to the desert.'

Pijaji said, 'Why did you have to tell him? We really wanted to take you.'

'Yes, I know,' said the boy.

Then Pijaji said, 'All right, we'll stay here in the station country.'

جرۍ

After that we set off eastwards to a place called Luck Bore. On the way my husband and the boy found some watermelon. They ate a lot of small ones that weren't ripe, then they found some big ripe ones and ate those too.

We turned south and came to the camp for the workers at Luck Bore. My older sister who had left the desert to walk to the cattle station before me, was among them. The next morning we joined the workers from Luck Bore on the station truck and went to Suzie Bore.

We began working with the group already there, and worked right through to the hot season. While we were there my sister became very sick and died. I was grief-stricken, hitting my head in sorrow for her. Soon after that we returned to Cherrabun and I cried for my sister with my relatives there.

The wet season came and we climbed onto the back of the station truck to go to the races at Fitzroy Crossing for the first time. Barney Lawford drove the truck. In the town the white people from the stations had set up their camp on the bank of the Fitzroy River, and we Aboriginal people were camped down on the sand below. There were lots of us there from Cherrabun, Gogo, and Christmas Creek stations. In the morning we went to see the horses racing with both Aboriginal and white riders.

One morning, a white woman came along to our camp. She had been watching our children swimming in the river, but they saw her and ran away frightened. She asked me, 'Whose are these children?' I said nothing as I didn't understand English. My aunty, Pingarri's mother, came to my aid, and said to the woman, 'They are children from Cherrabun Station.'

'Are they yours?'

'No, they are Jukuna's,' she said, nodding in my direction. 'She is looking after them.'

The woman said to me, 'May I take the children and put them into school?'

I didn't say a word. Then the woman went away to talk to someone else. Pingarri's mother asked me, 'Do you want to send your children to school?'

'I don't know, I'll talk to my husband,' I said.

I found him and said, 'A white woman has asked me if I want to send our children to school. Shall we send our children to school?'

'No,' he said. 'They might take them away away from us to another place. We'll look after them ourselves. Hide them so that she can't see them.' I hid them behind a paperbark tree near the river until the woman had gone.

It was also at that races time that I heard God's good news. It was a group of Aboriginal Christian leaders who told us. Their names were Limerick Malyapuka, Bandy Brown, Jack Jinakarli and Banjo Wirrinmara. It set me thinking, 'This seems like a good message they are telling us.' When the races had finished we went back to Cherrabun.

༄

I'll tell you about something good that happened. Pijaji and I thought that our family, who we'd left in the desert, were no longer alive. So, we pushed the memory of them from our minds, and worked on the station without thinking about them very much. You can imagine my shock when my sister and sister-in-law arrived at Christmas Creek Station. When I heard the news I was overjoyed and we went over to see them and cry with them. This is what had happened to them.

After we had left for the station country, it wasn't long before those two killers came from the south. They had spears, fighting sticks, boomerangs and other weapons. At first they just took over the family without doing any harm to them. But as time went on, they became violent and started killing people. In the end, they killed everyone in the family except two. One of those spared was my young sister. She had been frightened and, one night, secretly walked away from the camp. She carefully kept to grass-covered ground so that she left no footprints. They didn't find her.

My sister lived by hunting around the many jila she knew. One day, when she was heading north after quite a while alone, she came to a jumu where there was water to drink. She was still there when Pijaji's mother arrived, very weak from a spear wound. She had been with the family group when my sister ran away from the murderers. The next day they began walking north, but the old woman died before they had gone far. My sister returned to the jumu.

Later she saw the two murderers with their families coming towards the jumu and said to herself, 'I might as well give myself up.' When the two men found her, they were ready to spear her. But my husband's sister, who had been taken by one of the murderers for a wife, called out, 'Don't spear her, she's my sister-in-law! Let her live. Don't spear her. Have some pity and let her live.' So they let her live and she joined up with the family.

As they travelled on further north towards the stations, they heard cattle lowing in the distance. When they reached the bore called Parayipirri, they saw cattle everywhere. The two men said to the women and children, 'Stand in a circle around the cattle and close in on them so we can spear them.' But the women and children were too frightened to move. They had seen the big horns on those cattle. The two men got very angry with them for not doing what they were told, and whacked them all across the head.

Early the next morning they went back to the cattle and speared a bullock that was standing in the creek bed. They cooked it and ate the meat. Soon after that, men on horseback from the station galloped up and surrounded them. The people from the desert were frightened and crying. The stockmen took them all to Christmas Creek Station homestead and reported them to the manager. The two men were locked inside one of the buildings while the manager sent word for the police to come. They were taken to the jail in Fitzroy Crossing and kept there for a year.

Back at the station the Aboriginal workers got the rest of the family together. 'Where are you two from?' they asked my sister and sister-in-law. My sister-in-law said that her father's name was Maruwarnti and my sister told them her father's name – Kirikarrajarti. They knew straight away who the girls were, but they didn't know the others. These were the children of the two murderers and came from further south. Some of the old men at the station took the two men's daughters as their wives. They all became workers at Christmas Creek Station.

᪐

After we had been living at Cherrabun a good while people started talking about the station homestead. 'It's very close to the river and often gets flooded,' they said. So the decision was made for the homestead to be moved south to a part of the station that was on dry ground at Jukurirri Bore. This became the New Cherrabun. We all shifted over there to work.

While I was at New Cherrabun I had some of my children. My first and second sons were born there, on the station. The other two, a daughter then a son, were born in the hospital. They are all grown up now. A school was built at New Cherrabun, and we sent our elder sons and our daughter to the school when they were old enough.

We stayed working at that station for many years. When Christians came and told us God's good news, some of the men responded by leaving the law of the elders.

One wet season holiday my husband and I, with a woman I call mother and her husband and sister-in-law, set off to walk into Fitzroy Crossing to the Bible school at the mission. We slept two nights on the way, and on the morning of the third day we woke to see Christmas Creek in full flood.

One of our group, who has since passed away, said, 'What are we going to do? The water in this creek is very high. We can't swim across or we'll be drowned in the deep water.' Then he had an idea. 'Bring all your swags here,' he said. 'We'll tie them to sticks to make a kind of raft.' We did this, then we women and children lay face down on top of the swags, while the men swam, pushing the raft across the river to the north bank.

We walked on to Gogo Station where we spent the night with our relatives who were living there. The next morning we set off for Fitzroy Crossing. When we reached the south bank of the flooded Fitzroy River, we called out for the boat to come from the other side. We couldn't cross the river when it was in flood. There was no bridge for vehicles to cross, only a concrete road through the bed of the river, and when the river was in flood, they used to take us across by boat. On the north bank of the river, the big truck from the mission was standing waiting for us and the driver took us north to the mission. There we settled down and stayed for the holidays.

All of us were working happily at New Cherrabun until one day some of our people, who have since passed away, had a fight over something to do with the kitchen work. This made the manager angry and he gave us a hard time. Finally, the men said to one another, 'Let's go. Let's leave this manager. He can do his own work.'

Later, the manager paid us off with our rations. Some of the workers went into town in a truck to the races and stayed there. Others went on working on the station. The manager sent my husband and me and our children to Meda Station, near Derby, to work. Those who were left on New Cherrabun finally went to Fitzroy Crossing and stayed there, living in tents. The Kurnangki and Mindirardi communities didn't exist in those days. At that time there were only two stores in the town – one at the mission and another at the hotel. Aboriginal people used to get a form from the welfare office on the east side of the town, and then they had to take it to the mission store and get their rations with it.

My husband and I worked at Meda Station for a time, then we went to Derby and settled down to work there for a good while. My job was washing clothes for the children who lived in the mission hostel. My husband worked on Yeeda Station just out of town. We were a long way from the country we knew, so later on we returned to Fitzroy Crossing to stay.

∽

In my early years, when I lived in the desert, I didn't hear God. I wasn't aware of him or his word. Now I listen to him. I was walking around aimlessly in the darkness, but he brought me into the light. God is precious to me. I can't leave him. I have found something good for myself.

Over the years I have done a lot of work related to my language, Walmajarri. I learned to read Walmajarri and I have learned to write it too. With other people I translated some parts of God's word from English into Walmajarri. We carefully checked that work, then I read some of the translation onto cassettes. Those cassettes were sold to others so that they could hear God's word.

Another thing I did was teach some white people to speak a little Walmajarri. Later on I went to the adult education centre in Fitzroy Crossing, called Karrayili. There I began to learn English – writing and reading it, recognising the letters and words. Then I began painting pictures of my homeland on paper, the jila and the jumu, the rockholes and the sandhills. At first I painted small pictures and later on, large pictures. Over the last few years I have been painting very big pictures at the Mangkaja Arts Centre, some of which are sent away to the cities where people buy them.

A few years ago I went a long way from home on a trip overseas to Lyon, in France. I went there to tell the story of the huge painting called Ngurrara that was being shown in Lyon. It is a painting of all the important waterholes of our homeland. A great number of us belonging to that land painted it to show the government when we asked them for Native Title to our country. This painting has been sent to many parts of the world for people to see. I was glad to go to Lyon because I like seeing places that I have never seen before.

Now I teach children Walmajarri, and I really enjoy doing it. I teach them how to find bush foods and animals, and I teach them the names of the animals, such as goanna and fish. I teach them the names of the animals that live in the river country and that big goanna that belongs to the plains country. I also teach the children the names of other, smaller animals.

Lately, I've been thinking deeply about this important idea of returning south to the country where I was born. At the same time, I've been listening to what the government is saying – that the country belongs to them. So we have been discussing the idea of moving down to our country to live there, in our homeland.

Some of our people are saying that it is too far away from the town. Those of us who come from the desert say it is not far at all. Town people see our country as dry and waterless; to them it is just a lot of big sandhills and valleys. The desert people see it like this; yes there are high sandhills and valleys, but there are masses of food around the countless jila down there. There is no grog down there for people to drink, making them drunk and irresponsible. It's a good place to live far away from these things. This is the kind of discussion the desert people are having with the town people.

So I finish this short account of my life.

Top: Jukuna writing a story in Walmajarri, c1978

Bottom: Jukuna and Eirlys planning a Walmajarri lesson
for the Fitzroy Crossing school, c1992

Overleaf: Mining company's seismic lines in the desert

Left: Jukuna showing seed she has gathered, 1983

Above: Jukuna and Ngarta with their 'sister' Wawajarti (centre),
on a trip to their homeland

United Aborigines Mission
and surrounds, 1977

Kurrjalpartu
Ngarta Jinny Bent, 2001

Kurrjalpartu is a place we used to live at during the cold season and through
the hot season right up until the rains came. There was water
available right through the hot weather.

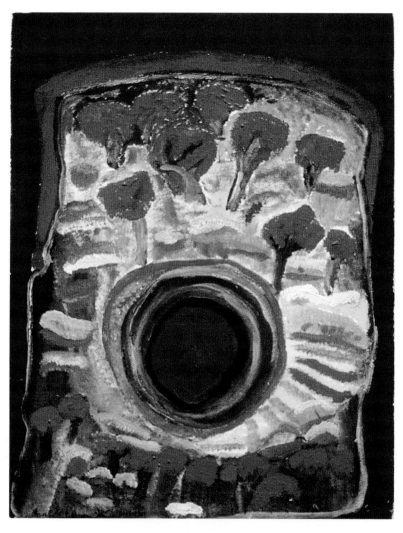

Wirrikarijarti
Jukuna Mona Chuguna, 2001

A jila near Wayampajarti, where we used to stay right through the hot
weather. There are turtujarti and kayala trees there.

Mitarta
Ngarta Jinny Bent, 2001

A salt flat not far from Tapu, on the way to Wanyngurla.

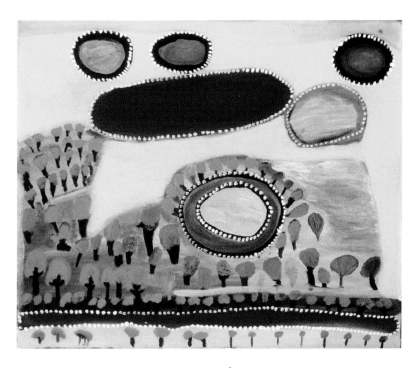

Wanyngurla
Ngarta Jinny Bent, 2001

There is water under the ground at Wanyngurla but it's salty and we can't
drink it. It is a place where we camped during the wet season and through till
the cold season. We got drinking water from a nearby soak.
There are many jurnta growing in that area and we ate lots of them
when we lived there.

Purtunjarti
Jukuna Mona Chuguna, 2002

A jumu. In the ngarrangkarni a young man drank water there. The young
man changed into the turtujarti tree near the jumu.

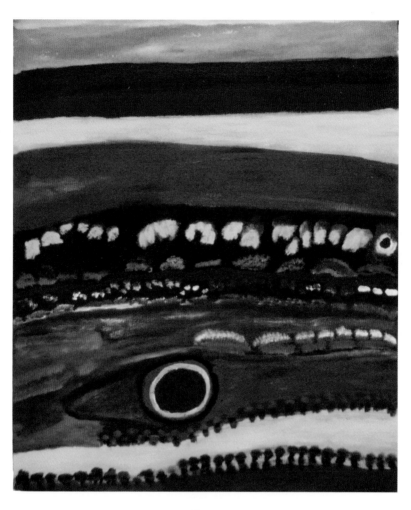

Tapu
Jukuna Mona Chuguna, 2002

We used to live at Tapu in the cold and hot seasons. There is good water
and lots of shady trees. We had to dig deep to get this water. We used to
get lots of food and meat when we stayed here.

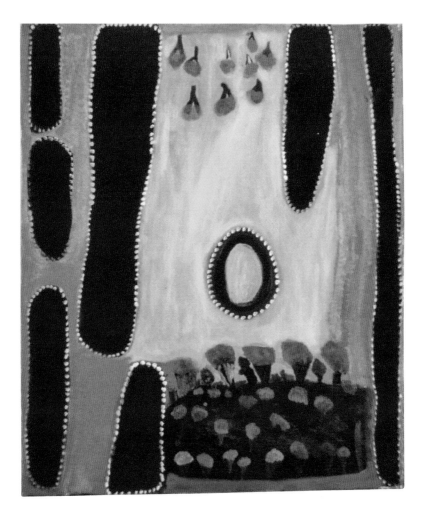

Pirrilanji
Ngarta Jinny Bent, 2002

This is the main place for the water serpent. In the Dreamtime it ate a man and vomited him back dead. From Wayampajarti we children used to visit this place and play there. Our mothers told us not to go there but we went anyway.

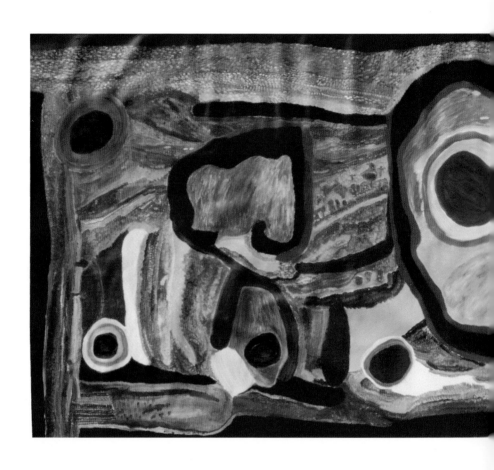

Wayampajarti
Jukuna Mona Chuguna and Ngarta Jinny Bent, 2000
(Painted during the Biennale de Lyon, France)

Wayampajarti is a living water spring. The water serpent lives in this one.
There is water here all year round. We dance and sing a corroboree about this
place. My father and two other old men got this song and dance in a dream.

Kurralykurraly
Mona Chuguna, 2001

We went to this jila in the hot season. Sometimes the water at
Kurralykurraly is good and sometimes it is salty. Even when it's salty we
can still drink it. We used to get desert nuts and other food there.
Animals used to come to drink and we would catch them for meat.

WANGKI NGAJUKURA JILJINGAJANGKA

JUKUNARLU PA YUTUKANI MINYARTI

Kurlampal marna ngunangani jarlu yapa jiljinga. Ngajukura ngarpu parla Wirtuka ngurrara. Jularni pila nganpayijarrarlu yini Kirikarrajarti nyanayirlarni. Kurriny nganpayijarra pila pirriyani jarlu ngarrangkarni. Nyanyala pilanya paja wirnkuma. Pajanani palunyanu kujangkurrajarra manawarntirla. 'Kkir! Kkir!' Marnani palu. Jularnila pila yini ngajukura ngarpu Kirikarrajarti nganpayijarrarlu. Jarriny parla wirnkuma.

Ngamaji ngajukura pa warntarni Japirnkajangka. Yangka pilanyan warntarni, nyanartijangkala pajapila jarrinypinya Mantartarla. Japingal pila tirrinyyani. Lapantinyala marnapilangurla lamparn yapa wurruwurru. Nyanartijangka

pukanyja karuwarrarni ngungkupinya ngajukurarlu ngarpungu
rawulmarni. Jularnila parla, 'Parnany, kunyungurla parlingurla
yapa pirriyani wurruwurru.' Nyanartijangka walimpa kantaralpala
pila warntarnani turtujartijangka jarriny Lantimangurla marnparni.

Nyanayirla pa ngunangani wurruwurru ngajukura papaji
kulipari. Layimirri ngajukura jaja paru luwarni miyingurni
manaputalngurni. Ngurru parla warntarni.

Ngajukura jamirti paji Japirnkakarraji. Jaja paji
kakarrangujangka, marrijangka. Karlangurlula warntarni
kakarra yanungurla. Ngawiji paji kayilungjangka Tapukarrajijaa
Wayampajartikarraji jilawarntiwarlanyjangka.

Nganampa marnal murrkurn marninwarnti, layi parri.
Kayanjangka ngamaji marnalu. Ngamajiwarlanyjangka palu
parriwarnti murrkurn, manga layi. Kanarlanykura ngamaji, pila
mangajaa piyirn. Kayanparni ngarpu marnapangu.

Wali jinanga narangalparnila marnal kitpungani
kayirrarajaa kurlirrara Mantartangurni. Mantarta pa jila, yarnta
kalpurtungajirtajarti.

Walimpa marna purlkajarrinya. Kuyi marna limpirri
pungani, yarnta ngiyarijaa kantamal marnanya pungani,
warlukarrpirnjuwaljaa jajalpi. Kamparnurla marna ngarnani.
Wali yarnta pajipila minijartijaa lungkura pungani jajangujaa
ngapurlurlu.

Wamarn marnal kitpungani ngapawarntirlal Mantartajangka.
Juljul marnalu ngarnani, tikirr Mantartakarti. Karlarrara
Nyalmiwurtukartijaa Lirrilirriwurtukarti, nyanartijangka
jumuwarlany Yirrjin, yarnta Warntiripajarra, Pirnturr.
Nyanartipurtarra marnalu warmarn kitpungani. Warntiripajarrarla
pa ngajukura ngawiji purangurlu manyjirni lurrujarti parranga.
Marlaljarrinyala.

Jilawarnti ngapawarnti marnanya julawu yiniwarnti. Wirtukajaa

Paparta, Mukurruwurtu, Warnti, Japirnka. Wali.

Makurrajarrinyjangka marnal yanani jilawarntiwarlanykarti kayirrara. Yiniwarnti marna julawu Walypa, Wayampajarti, Wirrikarrijarti, Kurralykurraly, Wanyngurla, Tapi, Kurrjalpartu, Wiliyi, Kayalajarti.

Yitirlaljangka makurra marnalunya warntarnani minyartiwarnti puluruwarntijaa miyiwarnti nyarrjarti, puturu, ngujarna, nyalmi, manyarl, jiningka, purrjaru, karlji, jalirr. Yarnta wamawarnti marnalu warntarnani makurra, wirijarti, jarnturntu, pirtiyamarta.

Yarnta marnalunya parranga warntarnani karlayin, lungkun, yiriwarra, tajitaji, malirrajangka. Malirrajangka pa nyanarti mungkunga nguniny kaninykaniny. Piyirn palurla yanani rakararla malangujarti. Lananila palu mungku, kanarlany kanarlany palu warpungani, kanarlany kanarlany palu warrapurru turnmanani. Tikirrjawurlu palu nukarnini warpungani. Tikirrkanganila palu kaniny ngalungkurra, purangurlala palu parntukanani. Lanani lalkawurra murrkamurrkala ngunangani. Ngarnanila palu wulyu pukarr.

Miyi ngarlka parla kujawurlurra parrangawujaa makurrawu ngunangani. Ngarnani marnalu nira. Parrangarlurra pa karrilany ngijirrimpil.

Minyartiwarnti palu kuyiwarnti yangka marnalu pungani nyurlkulku, mingajurru, marrany, waltaki, marliri, kunkuturru, parnaparnti, warna, jarany, lungkura, minijarti, ngirnu.

Wali kujartikarra kujartikarra, ngapawarlany ngapawarlany, jilawarntirlajaa jumuwarntirlajaa jiwariwarntirlajaa warrnganwarntirla marnalu kitpungani kuyi pungukarra yarnta miyijaa puluru warntarnukarra.

Yarnta yitirlaljangka wulyujangka paja puluru palu turtapungany. Ngapa pa purlkajangka wururu, pajakarrajangka manya warntalany ngapangu puluruparrtu puluruparrtu. Yarnta yitirlalwarlanyja manya warntalany yapalmarta ngapangu. Ngapajangka wulyujangka marnal munyal yutukarralany walimpapurru warntarnurla.

Kujartikarra marnalu yutukanani munyal. Luumanani marnalurla juranyjangka jarrja, yarnta jalngu marnalu warntarnani. Patarn kaninymarrangu marnalurla yutukanani. Mana marnalu pajanani tiwarlji. Wali watipirrapirra marnalurla yutukanani. Wanyjanani marnalu nyanartiwarnti puluruwarnti walimpapurru mananga kankarni tiwarljirla karntinga munyal.

Yarnta marnalu kurrkunga yutukanani. Walimpa marnalurla tikiyanani miyiwarntiwarlanypaliny wirlmanani. Purlpungani marnalu kurrkungajangka. Nyanartijangka jamurtu marnalunyanta lukurrpungani ngapangu. Kamparnanila marnalu warlunga. Nyanartijangka luwarnani marnalu, ngarnanila marnalu wuru.

Piyirntu palurla warrinyani parranga kuyiwu. Nyanartijangka yakapiri palurlanyan pungani jinapurru. Nyanayirlu pa piyirn kalypajanani jina kirtilywurra purangurlamarra. Kuyi palu lanani warltakijaa nyurlkulku, yarnta parnaparnti. Majirri pa wirlmarni ngayirta kitpungantarla.

Yarntarni marnal yanani ngapawarlanykarti. Kaparn marnal kirrarnani walmarta, ngapa wirlmarnani makurarlajangka. Karuwarrajarti marnal jakarnkarrangani. Kaparn marnal yukarnani pukanyja. Tarrapungani palu jarlany makurruwurra yukarnupurru. Rakarrarakarra wurnala marnal jakarnkarrakangani ngapakarti jilakarti.

Yarntarni marna wangkiwarlany julawu yapakura. Nguwakarlarn paja pinarriyungani puluru jarlarnupurru. Jajangujaa ngamajirlu pajapila pinarriyungani. Kurrapajarra paja warntarnani, nguwakarlarnta paja kaninymarrangu yutukanani kurrapajarra. Marnani paji, 'Kujarti man jalarnanku.' Marnani paji luutinykarrarla. Walimpawarlany marnarla pinarrijarrinya mangkurlajarrinyjangka. Nyanartila marna jarlarnani jirrkirl.

Narangalparni marna wangki julawu kuyi parla
kamparnupurru. Wali kuyiwurti marnanya pungani
lamparnwarnti, kurnka marnanya tikirrkangani. Warlula pajarrarla
jartkujirnani. Marnani paji jajangu, 'Yinti warntaji, kuyi parli
kampawu. Kujarti man kamparnanku yurnmiwurra.' Marnani paji,
'Ngajirta ngan warurrwarurr ngarnanta. Yurnmi man ngarnanku.'

Yarnta ngarlkawurti marnal mirntikanani tilinga warlunga. Wali
nyanarti marnal ngarnani warlu yawilji mirntikanujangka.

Yarnta kurlpa kunyarrkura marnal warntarnani. Kulmananila
marnalunyanangurla kurturtuwarntirla, nguwajawurlu marnal
turrkarra luwarnani pulparrwurra jamarnta. Nyanartila marnal
warlunga kamparnani yurnmiwurra, ngarnanila marnal.

౫

Jajarturlu paji jularnani kartiya ngirljarti. Kujarti paji jularnani
ngajukurarlu jajarturlu. Japirrjapirryungani marnarla ngininyju,
'Nganajiliny pa kartiya? Nungujiliny ngarta? Julaji.'

Nyantungu paji jularnani, 'Ngajirta. Miljarrajarti pa
kurrinyjarti.'

'Ya. Raljarti ngarta?'

'Yu, Raljartijal.'

'Ya. Kuyi marnarla pungani limpirri, nungula pajarra
julipungani marrarlalla. Minyartijiliny ngarta nungunungu?'

'Yu, Minyartijilinyjal,' Ngininyju marnarla japirrjapirryungani
kujarti.

౫

Walimpawarlany, yangka marna purlkajarrinya, jajangu
pajarranya jinjinyinya. Pulurula pajarrarla kangani nganykuru.
Nyantuwarlanyju parla yiparnani kuyi ngajukurawu ngamajiwu

karlarrara. Kayan nganyanta yangarra pirriyantarla munga parlanyanta mali ranyji.

Mali palunyanangu yutukanani ngawijirlu takingu purnta lamparn manga. Marnani parla ngawijirlu, 'Minyarti mangu nyuntuwu mali. Yunganku manurla nganykuru kuyi kirtangarni mangu purlkajarriwu.' Ngumparnala palurla yungany manga nyanarti yapala martarlany parrijaa mangawurti. Nyanarti parla pirtinyparni yungany nyanarti nganpayi purntajangka, parriliny kajalkajal, mangala jirna.

Walimpawarlany pajarranya jukujini ngumparnakarti Pijajikarti. Yukarni marnalu. Ngaju marna karlinta purlka, nyantu pa mangawarlany lamparnmarta mangkurla.

Walimpawarlany marniny pajarrangu, 'Wurna parlipa yanku kayili mayarukarti. Kangku marnanya ngarpujaa ngamajiwarntijaa jaja ngawijijaa malijaa ngajukurajarra kartujarra, mapirrirni yarnta ngajukurawarnti rimpiwarnti. Paja marnanya jinpinya mangarriwarntijaa purluman kuyi yalayirla kartiyakura. Nukarni marnanya kangku, kayan ngarnanya wanyjarra piyirnkarrarla, wartangurni nganyalu pungka.

Pijaji pilangu pinarri ngunangani kuliparijarrawu. Nyanartila marnapangu marni. Pinakarrinya pinya nyantukurawarntirlu kurlangujangkawarntirlu palupinya lani Nganpayijaa ngamajinyankura.

Ngajukurarlu jajangujaa Pijajikurarlu jajangujaa ngamajijarrawarlanyju palurla marni, 'Wanyjarrku marnanpanya. Kirrarnanku marnalu nganampakurarla ngurrararla, kayan ngarnanpanya kangka. Wali marnanpanya wanyjarrku minyayarlarni ngurrararla nganampakurarla. Kayan ngarnanpanya kangka nyanartikarti mayarukarti. Marri marnapangurla. Yarra manta.' Ngajukura pa jaja parnanyjinyangu. Kayan ngarta marri yantarla. Kanajarti pa jitakkarra yanani. Ngajukurarlu ngajangu parla yakurrmarni wanyjanupurru wartangurni. Ngamaji jaa jajajaa ngaja. Yawiyijarrinya manyanangu. Wali lamala palu kirrarnani nukarni.

Wali makurrajangka larlilarlirla marnalu wurna jakarnkarra kanya kayili mayarukarti ngajukurajarra lamparrjaa ngunyarri, Pijajikura ngarpujaa ngamaji, layi manga pila kangani, ngajuwu paji mantirri. Nyanartiwarnti marnalu yani. Wali pikajarrinyurla marnalu yani kayili.

Yani marnalu Yarntayi tirriny kayirrarni. Kaparn marnal yukarni. Rakarrarakarrarla marnal wurnajarrinya Larrilarrikarti. Jarti marnalu nyanya ngapangajirta, marri pa kaniny ngujangurra. Tirrinyyani marnalu Pilyjiwurtukarti jumuwarlanykarti. Ngarnungkarranya marnal wurnangurni. Karuwarrajarrinya marnapangurla kaparn ngurrala marnalu yukarni.

Kumanta marnal turtapinya, nyanyala marnal pamarr Jarrngajarti ngurrpangu. Turtangkarrakanya marnal, pamarra marnal nyanya ngapa najinga. Purlumanwarnti palu nyanyayirla karrinyani ngapanga. Jarlu marna nyanya nyanarti purluman, kurlirra jiljinga, pinarrila marnarla. Ngarnila marnal, ngapa nyanarti kayirrarni Jinpirimpirirlal marnal tirriny yani.

Pirriyanila marnalu puwunga. Kurlirrara marnapanya yutukani yungkanga pukanyja. Tirrinyyani manyanangurla wurturlanyjartikarti. Pinarri palurla ngujangurra, jarlu palu nyanya Pijaji. Kirrarnani palu wurturlanyjarti. Purrkungu pinya martarnani parnanyjarra kurriny. Jularni parla parnanywarlanyju, 'Yangkartu pa piyirn pirriyani.'

Papajanila parla parnanywarlanyju. 'Mirnu yananawu. Julawu pajin wangki.'

'Ngajirta pawu. Ngajukura marna walakujpurru kanyangurra.'

'Kangkaji mirnu,' marni parla parnanyju. Miyiliny parla yinya miyijaa kuyi ngilyki.

'Yu,' marni parla. 'Warra marnangu pirrikangku.'

Pirrikanya marnapanya ngajujaa ngarpujaa ngamaji pukanyja. Wali lungani marnalunyan.

Jularni parla ngajukurarlu purrkungu, 'Minyarti pajipila, ngajukurajarra, ngarpujaa ngamaji. Minyarti paji ngajuwu kartu.' Parnanyju parla japirryinya, 'Nganakura nyanarti marnin? Julaji.' 'Jaja parla Nakayi. Yani pa Pamarrjartikarti kayili jarlu.'

'Ya. Ngajukura paji jaja.'

Walimpawarlany marni parla purrkuwu Pijajirlu, 'Wurna marnalu yanku kayirrara Jukurirrikarti puwuwarlanykarti. Nyaku marnarla kakajpurruwu.'

'Ya, wali pawu, yantanyanta. Nyakarla kakajpurruwu.'

Wali wurnajarrinya marnal.

Pirriyani marnalu puwuwarlanyja Jukurirrirla. Marni marnapangu ngajukurarlu purrkungu, 'Kirranyjalu minyartirla ngalunga. Nyaku marnarla ngumparnajpurru.'

Yanila parla, marni parla kakanyankurawu, 'Ngumparnajpurru marna pirrikanya ngajukura yirna.'

'Ya. Nyaku marna kuwarrirni.'

Purparnila. Marni parla, 'Minyarti marna ngajukura ngumparnajpurru pirrikanya.'

Kayilungu kirrarnukujirni. Lunganila palunyanu ngayiwarntirlu.

Miyila marnapanya yinya. Yukarni marnalu layi ngurra.

Wali marni parla ngajukurarlu purrkungu, 'Wanyjarrku marnanpinya ngumparnarra. Minyayirla manpila kirralku kajalu.'

Marnila parla wartangurni, 'Pa. Yanku marna mapirrijarti.' Yani pila kankarral tayingkakarti. Nyanya ngapa kankarninyirra tayingkarla wuru yukarnjangka ngurrpangujal. Murrula tikilaparnila karrarta, mungkula warntarni. Marni, 'Wawu! Ngaju marnawu pirriyani!' Mungkujawurlu luwarni

ngurrpangurrparlu. Ngaru manyan jiwupinya. Ngajirta pa jarlu
nyangantarla kujartijiliny kurlampal. Kula parla nyantungu marni
kalpurtujartirni.

Kalpartu pa jilawarntirla nguniny, ngapa pa martalany. Puju
ngayi kanginypungany, walypala parlanyanta turtapungany wirrilyi.
Pilyurr ngarta tapantarla. Wali marni parla nyanartikarrijirlu,
'Ngajirta pa nyanarti jila. Yarr pa ngapa warntarni mijiyintu
kartiyakurarlu kaninyjangka. Pa, tikiyanku marna jurnpurrkarti
mapirrijarti.'

Ruwa pajarra yani kayirra puwuwarlanykarti Purlkartujartikarti.
Nyanayirla palu warrkammarnani ngapapurru tayingka
piyirnwarntirlu. Pirriyanila pajarra pukanyja. Yukarni pajarra
layi ngurra. Kumantajarti nyanya pajarranya Paaniluputtu
warrkammayintu rapukaajirlu. Marni manyanangu
warrkamayinwarntiwu, 'Warntawu marna nyanarti boy,
warrkammalku pajirla ngajunga.'

Wali pajarranya warntarni. Ngurtinga pajarra parayani, kanyala
pajarranyalu kayili warrkamkarti. Nyangani marnanya manawarnti.
Kula palu pupururni laparnani. Ngaju marna parntakarrinyani
ngurtinga karrarta ngurrpangurrpa.

Kanya pajarranyalu kayirrara pirrakarti Warrpipakarti. Pajanani
palu puwuj parrikpurru piyirnwarntirlu. Ngajarrarlu pajarra
kamparnani puluwa kukumanjarrarlu Pajimankurarlu kartungu.
Nyangani marna ngurrpangu kurtayimanujangka puluwa.

Yarntarni pajarranyalu kanya ngurtijarti kurlirrara Jukurirrikarti
tikirrparni. Purpankanya pajarrapinya jamirlangu Pijajikura
ngamajijaa yirna Timpakirikkarti. Wali mangarri marnalu ngarnani
nyanayirlarni. Yangka pajarra kurlilangu pirriyani puwunga.
Nyanayirlarni marnalpinya ngangamarni mantirrirlangu wayinurtu
ngajukurawu purrkuwu parla ngamaji, yarnta Japirirrikura.
Wali lungani marnalpilangu yawiyirlu. Nyanartikarra ngajirta

pila ngumparnarra kalkarrajarra kirrarnantarla lukajarti. Ngurrpa
marnalurla ngunangani. Jarlu kurlampal jilawarntirla ngajirta palu
martarnantarla kalkarrarlu luka.

Layimirri manyanangu ngapa ngarla warntarni warrkammayintu
Paaniluputtu Kurijmijpurru tawunjangka. Ngarnanila palu
wangartawurrra. Wali warpijngarni palu. Nganamparlu marnalunya
nyangani ngurrpangu. Rayinjarrinyala marnal ngurrpawarnti.
Pungkarla ngarnapanyalu turangkinpalarlu.

Walimpa marnalpinya kanya ngumpanarra kalkarrajarra
mayarukarti Jarraparnkarti kayili, yapajarra mapirrirni. Pirriyani
marnalu kayili mayarurla. Nyanganila marnapanyalu ngayiwarntirlu
pirriyanjangka. Layi marnalu nginyjirrikani. Lunganila
marnapangurlurla nginyjirrikanungurla. Kirrarnani marnalu paja
piyirn.

Nyanartijangka juju marnapangulu yinparni Julurru.
Mayarujangka marnapanyalu kanyapakul karla. Makartala
marnapangulurla yutukani jurlunga. Kayan ngarnal warrpunyakarla.
Nguwa marnal nyangani kaninyparral. Nyanartijangka kanya
marnapanyalu pirntirrikarti karuwarrarla, jujula palu kartijpani.
Marni marnapangulu 'Munta tarrpartalunyanu. Karrpilikanyja
nganta.' Nyanya marnalunya kukukumarnujangka. Nyanartijangka
yinparnani palu kakarrara manyanngajirta. Kamparnani palunyan
warlujawurlu. Nyanartijangka kumantajartila palunyan yungani
mangarrijaa kuluwujwarnti.

꒰꒱

Nyanartikarra marna jalarramiparni nyanya kartiya ngurrpangu
Pinapinakarrinya marna, 'Aa nyanarti pa kartiya ngirljarti.'
Nyanti pa nganpayi yini parla Kuripina, maja marnapangu. Rajin
marnapanya yungani nyantungu.

Wali warrkammarnani pajarrarla majawu nyanayirlarni

mayururla yitilalwarnti paja kitangarni pajarrarla pinarrijarrinya
warrkamku.

Jarlu marnarla ngurrpa ngunangani nanikutku ngamarna
nyulypungupurru. Majangu parla marni parnanyku, 'Yungkarla
warrkam marnin nyanarti nanikut.'

'Yu,' marni parla. Wali purpani paja parnanyju.

'Marlamanku pajan nanikut,' marni paji.

Ngajungu marna pinapinakarrinya, 'Minyarti pa kunyarr

Marni paji parnanyju, 'Marrki man tarrpartawu jina. Kanyji
nganta jinangu.'

Nyanartijangka nyulypungungurla marnal ngamarna kangani
kaninykaninyjurra pakitwarntirla mayarukarti wirtijurrmanupurru
jirajaa ngamarna ngarnupurru.

Yarnta marnarla pinarrijarrinyani purlumanukurawu jupku.
Wirtijurrmanani marnal jira warlungajangka pakitwarntirla
jawutajarti. Purtkujirnanila marnal ngurtinga japalla.
Nyanartijangka kutikananila marnal nyanarti kankarnimarrangu.
Kumantajartila marnal jup junjumanani piyirnwarntiwu
yungupurru kuluj wajimmanupurru.

Yarnta kanarlany warrkamwarlany marnal turakjangka
muntumuntukangani tuwakarti nganapartu-nganapartu
kaninykaninyjurra. Wali.

Nyanartijangka purlumanukarti marnapanya kangani
kartiyarlu. Luwarnani purlumanu, marninwarntirlula marnal
jungarnurla tarratarrapungani kankarral ngurtikarti. Tikirrkangani
mitawujkarti, maparnani marnal julkjawurlu ngarnupurru warra.

Yarnta wangkiwarlany marna julawu. Maparnani
marnal pulayinku turam parpjartijawurlu, nyaku manyanta
pulayinjawurlu. Nyanartijangkala yutantinyani. Nyanartiwarntiwu
marnarla pinarrijarrinya warrkamku yangka marna kurlangu
pirriyani jiljingurni.

Wali nyanayirlarni marnalunya ngangamani ngurturrwarnti
nganampakurawarnti Jarraparntarni. Ngurrpa marnalurla
ngunangani kujartijilinyku mimiwu kurlampal. Ngajukura
lamparr nyanayirlarni marlaljarrinya. Nyana pa ngajukuraliny
purrku marlaljarrirla. Ngarpukurajangkarla manyanta warntarni
pilyurr. Yinyala parla wanji ngajukura purrku. Ngaju marna yara
ngunangani mimingajirta. Yapawarnti marnanya ngampurrikanani
ngumuwarnti Pali, Japirirri, Nyija.

Wali pakulkanyala ngajukura purrku jarna ngurrawarlanyjurra,
ngajukura lamparr marnal yartajpani. Kumantawarlany
marnal wurna jakarnkarranya pukanyja kurlirrara tumaj palu
jarntuwarnti kirrarnani. Lamakujirla ngarnapanyalu. Ngajukura
purrku warrarni manyjarr, yuntala marnal yanani. Parrijaa
manga ngumujarra mapirri pajarrapinya kangani. Ngurra marnal
juntumani kaparn jiljinga.

Kumantajarti marni parla purrkungu marranyanjawurlu.
'Parri kangku marnanta ruwa, kalparrku pajin warntawu.' Purrku
ngajukura warrarni kirrarnani manyjarr.

'Ya,' marni parla parringu. Kalparrkukura kirlingirri pila
parlipinya. 'Parri, takurryantarla kurrapa!' Parri takurrpinya,
karlarnani parla, kurrapala pajani kalparrkurlu. 'Warawu, warawu,
karrkarr paja pajani.' Nungujartijarrinyala. Wali purrkungula
manya warntarnani lukangajangka pajajinyangu kalparrkuwarnti.
Kamparnurlala pila ngarnani kuyi.

Kanarlanywarnti palu jarntuwarnti wartangurni pirriyani
layi purrkujaa marninwarnti murrkurn nyanayirla jiljinga.
Nyanartijangka kumantawarlany marnalpinya wanyjani
wartangurni, layiwarlany mimijarti jurumanani.

Marni marnalurla, 'Yanku ngarlipa kurlirrara.'

Parnanyju marni mimijawurlu, 'Ngajirta. Wanyjarrku pajanta minyayirlarni. Lama marna kirrarnanku.'

Parringu parla marni, 'Kangku marnantalu ngamaji mapirri.' 'Ngajirta, kaparn ngarna wanti.' Parringu parla lungani mapirri kangupurru.

Kurlirrara marnalu yanani. Pirriyani marnal Jukurirrirla karuwarrarla. Yutantinyala marnal ngalunga. Kamparnani marna kakaji. Nyanyala ngajukurarlu purrkungu wangkarna mananga kirrarnjangka lamparn. Marni parla parriwu, 'Parri, pungku pajin wangkarna lamparn.' Laparnkarranya manyanta parri. 'Parakujiwu manyanta mananga, pungku pajin wangkarna.' Parringu pinyala manajawurlu. Kamparnurlala pila ngarnani.

Nyanartikarrarni marnani parla ngajukurarlu ngumparnarlu, 'Parri, kangku pajarrarnanta kurlirra tikirr jilawarntikarti. Wali marna mimi wantinya minyayirla mayarurla.'

Parringu parla marni, 'Ngajirta, kayan ngarna yanta kurlirra, marri pajirla.'

Yani parla parri ngarpuwarlanyku.

Marni parla, 'Yirna , yangka pajapila kurlirra tikirr kangku.'

Purrku kulkuru kirrarnani.

Parringu parla jurtungu marnani, 'Kangku pajapila kurlirra.'

Jangkumani manyanta purrkungu. 'Ngajirta. Kayan nganta yanta. Lama manta kirrarnanku minyayirla. Yarnta ngarta mimijarri.'

'Ya. Wali pawu. Julawu marnarla ngajukurawu Pijajiwu. Ya.'

Tikiyanungurla parla jularni, 'Yangka parlipanya marrkukani ngarpungu.'

Pijajirlu parla marni, 'Nganapurru manurla jularni, parri? Wurnajal pajarrarnanta kangkarla.'

'Ya. Wali pawu.'

Marni parla Pijajirlu, 'Lama parlipa kirrarnanku minyayirla.'

～

Nyanartijangka marnalu yanani kakarra, watimilin pila parlipinya kaparn. Ngarnani pila kurnkawarnti murrjurl, yarnta purlkapurlka pukarr.

Nyanartijangka kurlirrara marnal yani, pirriyanila marnalunangurla warrkammayinwarntirla Lakpuwarla. Ngajukura ngapurlu mapirri kirrarnani nyanayirla. Kumantajarti marnapanyal parakujirni turakja Jujipuwakarti.

Wali marnal warrkammarnani nyanayirla larlilarlirla, larlilarlijangka parrangajarrinya. Nyanartikarrarni ngajukura ngapurlu mimijangka marlaljarrinya. Lungani marnarla pajanurla. Wurnajarrinya marnalu Jarraparnkarti.

Nyanartijangka marnalunya piyirnwarntiwarlany parakujirni rijijkarti turakja yawarta nyangupurru ngurrpangu. Paanilapattu pa turayipimkujirnani turak. Juntumanani palu martuwarrarla kankarnimarrangu kartiyawarntirlu ngurra yukarnupurru. Nganampa piyirnwarnti marnal kaniny martuwarrarla walyarrarla yukarnani paja Jarraparnjangka jaa, Pamarrjartijangka jaa, Kurungaljangka mapirrirni. Kumantajarti marnal yanani yawarta nyangupurru pupurulaparnjangka piyirnjartijaa kartiyajarti.

Layimarri kumantajarti walyarrarla pirriyani layi marnin kartiya. Nyanya manya yapawarnti nyumukanujangka. Rayin nyanyala palu kartiya, laparnkarranya palu.

Japirryinya paja, 'Nganakura palu nyanarti yapawarnti?'

Ngaju marna kulkuru karrinyani, kayan ngarna pinakarrirla Yingkilij. Ngajukurarlu Pingarrikurarlu ngamajirlu paja marlamani.

Marni parla, 'Nyanarti palu Jarraparnjangkawarnti yapawarnti.'

'Nyuntukura ngangulu nyanartiwarnti yapawarnti?'

'Ngajirta. Jukunakurawarnti palurla. Nyantungu manya ngampurrikarralany.'

Marni paji, 'Kangku ngarnanya kuulkarti yapawarnti jalaaliny?'

Ngaju marna kulkuru karrinyani. Kartiya nyanarti
wurnala yani.

Marni paji wartangurn, Pingarrikurarlu ngamajirlu, 'Yapawarnti
nganunya yipawu kuulkarti?'

'Julawu marnarla ngajukura purrku,' marni marnarla.

Yani marna, marni marnarla purrkuwu, 'Yipawu ngarlinya
yapawarnti kuulkarti?'

Ngajukurarlu purrkungu paji marni, 'Ngajirta. Marri nganya
yap kangka ngurrawarlanykarti. Martarnanku parlinya lama.
Ranyjikujiwu manunya, nyaka nganya.'

Nyanartijangka marnanya mawulpirrirla ranyji yutukani
kitangarni nyanarti marnin yap yani.

Yarnta pinakarrinyani marna Ngarpukura wangki wulyu
nyanartirla rijijja. Kurnkurnwarntirlu purlkawarntirlu
marnapangulu wangki wulyu jularnani Ngarpukura yiniwarntirlu
Malyapuka, Purrkuli, Jinakarli, Wirrinmarra.

Nyanartikarra marna pinapinakarrinyani kunyungurla palu
wulyu wangki jularnana. Wali rijijjangka marnal Jarraparnkarti
tikiyani.

⁓⁓

Julawu marnanyirrangu minyarti wangki. Kula pajarranya
wanyjani piyirnngajirtarlarni jilawarntirla. Nyanartijangka
pajarra rukarnurla warrkammarnani mayarurla ngangangu.
Nyanartijangka karrpirlmarnila marnapilangu pirriyanujangkawu.
Jularniliny pajilu minyarti wangki. Wirriyajarrinyala marnapilangu.
Yanila pajarrapilangu Kurangalkarti nyangupurrujaa lungupurru.
Kujarti palu ngunangani.

Wartangurni pila pirriyani kulijarti pirlajarti. Kurlata, kuturu,
karli, mukurru nganapartu nganapartu pilanya kanya. Wali

pilanya warntarni wulyuwulyu. Yarnta pilanyanangu kurtkarrinya
wanjijangkawu. Nukarni manya pinya, kurriny pinya jarnmarni,
ngajuwumipa marnarlanyanta wanji. Yukangal pa yirrpyirrpkarra
yani pukanyja pukanyja ranyji rayin pikajarrinyurla.

Wamarn kitpungani jilawarntirlal. Walimpawarlany
wurnajarrinya kayili. Jumu parlipinya ngapa. Walila kirrarnani
kitangarni ngunyarri manyanta pirriyani lanurlakanujangka
limijarti. Pirriyani pilanyanta kuliparijarra wartangurni.
Kajaluwarlanyparni marlaljarrinya ngajukura ngunyarri jamurn
pila pirriyani nyanartijarra kuliparijarra.

Nyanya pinya, marni parlanyanu muntanga, 'Jamulu
marnanyan pika yungku.' Wali, marni pilangu ngajukurarlu
mantirrirlu, 'Ngajirta nganpila lanta. Ngajukura paji mantirri.
Wanyjarra pila wanji. Ngajirta nganpila lanta. Wanyjarra pila wanji
yawiyi.' Marni pilangu mantirrirlu, 'Ngajirta nganpila pungka.'
Nyanartijangka pila wanyjani wanji, mapirrikujirni pinya.

Kayili palu yani. Pinakarrinya palunya purlumanu
murumarnujangka. Parayipirrirla, ngapanga palunya nyanya
karrinyujangka kujangkurrajarra. Marni pilanyanangu,
'Tinylapanyjalurla wamarn' Yangka palu jatajatalani
rayin. Nyanyaliny palunya purlka wunjarti. Kulijarrinyala
manyanangu layiwarlany, kanarlany mapirrirni. Pinyala pilanya.
Nyanartijangkarlu pilanyanangu kulijarrinya.

Kumantajarti rakarrarla palurla tikirr laparni, lanila palu
kaniny walyarrarla ngapanga nyanarti purlumanu. Kamparnurlala
palu ngarnani. Piyirnwarnti palu wamarn laparni yawartajarti
mayarukarraji, rukukani palunya walyarrarla, warntarni palunya.
Lunganila palu karrarta. Warntarni palunya, kanyala palunya
mayarukarti. Majawuliny palurla marni. Martarnani palupinya
nganpayijarra nyanartijarra kaninykaniny, limpawula palurla
yiparni majanga. Kanyala pinya limpajartikarti. Nyanayirla pinya

martarnani jayilla layiwu yitilal.

Wartangurn palunya nyantujarrakurawarnti marurrpinya, japirrmani palupinya marninkujarra, 'Wanyjarrajangka manpila nyurrajarra?' Ngarpu parlanyan layingu jularni yini Maruwarnti. Kanarlanyju parlanyan ngarpu yini jularni Kirikarrajarti. Wali nginyjirrikani palupinya jarntujarra. Kanarlanywarnti kuliparijarrakura ngajirta palunya nginyjirrikarrarla.

Warntarnila palunya ngumparnawarntirlu kurntalwarnti kuliparijarrakurawarnti.

Wali warrkam palunya yinya nyantujarrakurawarnti mayarurla nyanartirla Kurungalla. Wali.

❦

Nyanartijangka marnalu pinapinakarrinya mayarupurru, 'Minyarti pa martuwarrarla mayaru ngapakurarla.' Nyanartila marnalpakulkanya pulparrkarti mayaru nyanayirla Jukurirrirla.

Kujartikarra marnanya martarni yapawarnti. Kurrinywarlany pila wuujpilngurnipakul palkangajarrinya, parri kajalurnjangka, parriwarlany wartangurni. Kurrinywarlany pila wuujpilla palkangajarrinya parrijaa manga. Nyanartijangka palu purlkajarrinya.

Nyanartijangkarlu palu mayaru Jukurirrirla ngartakpani kuul yapapurru pinarriyungupurru. Yapawarnti marnalunya martarnani kuulla, ngajukurawarnti mapirrirni parrijarrajaa manga. Warrkammarnani marnalu nyanayirlarni mayarurla lama yitilalwarnti paja. Nyanartijangka ngarpukurala marnapangulu jularnani wangki wulyu Ngarpukurajartiwarntirlu yangka palu piyirnwarntirlu palu wanyjani luwu purrkuwarntikura.

Layimarri marnalu yani yitilal Pirturayikarti Ngarpukurakarti. Ngajujaa purrku ngajukura marnalu yani, ngajukura ngamajiwarlany, ngumparnanyankurajaa nyantukura rimpi mapirri marnalu yani. Kaparn marnalu yukarni ngurrajarra kurriny. Kumanta marnalu turtapinya, nyanya marnalu kuparlaparla kurungal martuwarra.

Marni marnapangu ngurturru, 'Nyapartujarriwu parlipa, ngapakata purlkajinyangu. Kayan ngarlipa jawumanyja, yurranti ngarlipa ngapanga purlkanga. Kalukuwarnti kutakuta kangarnilu. Karrpiwu parlipa mananga kalpiya.' Wali lapartwantinya marnalu kankarnimarrangu kalukurla. Kayirnikayirni marnapanyapila jawukanya piyirnjarrarlu.

Yanila marnalu Pamarrjartikarti. Nyanayirla ngurra marnalunyanangurla yukarni jarntuwarntirla. Kumantawarlanyja marnalu jakarnkarrakanya pirturayikarti. Kulirnikulirni marnalurla pawupawumarnani pawutku martuwarrarla. Kayan ngarnalu tirriny yanta ngapangal purlkangal. Ngajirta parla jarrnga warntarri ngunarla ngurtiwu, jarlu pa ngunangani nguwangal jiminj. Jarlu marnapanyalu kangani puwutjawurlu ngapangal purlkangal. Kayilungujarti marnapangu karrinyani purlka ngurti mijinjangka. Kayilila marnapanya kanya mijinkarti. Nyanayirla marnalu wali kirrarnani lama niyirnparni yaliti.

Nyanartijangka marnalu wulyuwulyu warrkammarnani Jukurirrirla. Walimpawarlany kulila palunyan pinya ngurturrwarntirlu kijinngurni. Nyanartijangka marnapangu kulijarrinya majangu. Marrarnani marnapanya. Wali marni palurlanyan piyirnwarntirlu, 'Wurna parlipa yanku. Wanyjarrku parlipa nyanarti maja. Nyantungu parlanyan warrkammarnanku jintanga.'

Nyanartijangka rajin marnapanya yinya majangu. Kanarlanywarnti palu ngurtijarti laparni rijijkarti. Nyanartila palu lamajarrinya Pijrayirla. Kanarlanywarntirlu palu warrarni warrkammarnani. Ngajarra pajarranya yiparni Mitakarti. Wartangurni palu yani Pirturayikarti. Kirrarnanila palu

kalikujartipakul. Mayaru pa ngajirta ngunarla Kurnangkijaa
Mintirarri. Tuwa nguja kayili mijinta yarnta kakarra papilikajja.
Mirlimirli palu warntarnani apijjangka kayili kapumankura,
kanganila palu mijintuwakarti warntarnupurru rajin.

Warrkammarnani pajarra Mirtanga, nyanartijangka
pajarrapakulyani tawunkarti Purulakarti. Nyanayirla marnalu
niyirnparni warrkammarnani. Yapawarntikura kuluwujwarnti
marnalunyanangu wajimmarnani. Ngajukurarlu purrkungu
pa warrkammarnani tiijinta Yitanga. Marriwarnti pajarra
warrkammarnani. Walimpala pajarra tikiyani Pirturayikarti
niyirnparni.

ॐ

Jarlu marna ngajirta ngarpu pinakarrinyantarla jiljinga. Yarr marna
nganga ngunangani. Ngajirta marnarla pinarri ngarpukurawu
wangkiwu. Jalarra marna ngarpu pinakarrilany. Wali Ngarpungu
paja tilingakujirni mungangajangka wampalkarra kitpunganjangka.
Ngarpu paji marulu, kayan ngarnajin wanyjarra. Wulyu marnajin
parlipinya.

Wali marna warrkammarnani Walmajarri ngajukura wangki.
Pinarrijarrinya marnarla ritimkujirnupurru wangki Walmajarri
mirlimirlirlajangka. Yarnta marnarla pinarrijarrinya lanupurru.
Nyanartijangka marnal Ngarpukura wangki kurnakkujirnani
Yingkilijjangka Walmajarrikarti. Nyanartirni wangki marnal
jirrkirlikanani. Kajittala marna wangki ritimkujirnani.
Jalimkujirnanila marnalunya kajitwarnti piyirnwarntiwarlanyja
Ngarpukura wangki pinakarrinyupurru.

Yarnta marnanya pinarriyungani kartiyawarnti Walmajarri
jarluwarlany, wali wangki kutakuta.

Kanarlany wangki, marna warrkammarnani Karrayilirla kuul.
Karrayili kuulla marnarla pinarrijarrinyani Yingkilijku. Wangki

marna lanani, yarnta marna ritimkujirnani, nampala marna nginyjirrikanani. Maparnanila marna mirlimirlirla ngurrara jilawarntijaa jumuwarnti. Yarnta jiwariwarntijaa jiljiwarnti marna pirtimanani lamparnlamparnpaliny purlkapurlkala. Nyanartijangka Mangkajarlala marna piyintingkujirnani purlkapurlka. Yiparnani marna pamarrpurru ngajukura piyinting.

Walimpawarlany marna marri yani wupajiyi Liyankarti. Waanya marna purlka ngurrara piyinting. Wulyumarni marnarla nyangupurru ngurrawarlany ngurrpangu.

Jalarrawarlany yapala marnanya pinarriyungany. Wulyumalany marnarla. Pulurujaa kuyi jinamanupurru marnanya pinarriyungany. Yarnta ngana kuyi yini, kakajijaa kapi ngapakarraji martuwarrakarrajiwarnti. Kakaji pa pirntirrikarraji. Wali kanarlanywarnti kuyiwarnti mapirrirni lamparnlamparn. Minyartiwarnti marnanya pinarriyungany yapawarnti.

Jalarrawarlany marna pinapinakarrilany tanyjingal. Minyarti pajirla purlka ngajukurakarti ngurrarakarti tikirryanupurru kurlirrara. Jalarrawarlany marna kapumankura wangki pinakarrilany. Ngurra nyanarti parla nyantukura kapumankura. Nyanartijangka marnalu yirrikanana piyirnwarntirlupakul yanungurla kirrarnupurru ngurrararla.

Kanarlanyju piyirntu palu nyangany marri. Piyirntu jilakarrajirlu nyangany marnpa. Piyirntu mayarukarrajirlu palu nyangany pulparr ngapangajirta. Purlka manyanangurla jiljijaa parapara. Piyirntu jilakarrajirlu palu nyangany kujarti. Purlka parlanyanta jiljijaa parapara. Pulurupartu pulurupartu palu nguniny jilawarntirla paja. Ngajirta ngapa langa wangartawurrra ngarnupurru. Wulyu pa jarungkurra ngunangupurru. Minyarti wangki palunyanangu jilakarrajirlu yirrikanana mayarukarrijiwu piyirnku.

Wali ngajukura wangki kutarni marna pujumani.

THE WALMAJARRI
DIASPORA

When Walmajarri people left the desert, different groups headed out in different directions, more or less according to the proximity of their homelands to a particular settlement, station or mission. Those who lived to the west came out at La Grange, those further south of west, at Jigalong. Eastern Walmajarri moved towards the stations or Catholic missions at Balgo and Billiluna. The central and central-southern groups headed north in stages, eventually to come out at the cattle and sheep stations of the Fitzroy Valley. South of Walmajarri country lay more desert, the domain of other language groups, whose history was similar, yet different in particulars. These people too were drawn or forced into scattered settlements closer to their own homelands.

Each of the destinations in the Walmajarri diaspora lies in the country of a different language group: Nyangumarta at La Grange,

Martu at Jigalong, Jaru at Ringer's Soak, Nyikina at Noonkanbah. Mulan and Billiluna, among others, lie within Walmajarri country. Fitzroy Crossing, the small town where Jukuna and Ngarta's family eventually settled, along with the many other people who had worked on cattle stations, is Bunuba country. While the Bunuba people have perforce accepted the presence of Walmajarri, Nyikina and many other groups as settlers, squatters or refugees on their land, they remain its true custodians and owners. Bunuba people's rights to make decisions about their own country are not disputed by the other language groups, always, of course, discounting the white people, who make it their business to mind everyone else's. Nevertheless, even after two generations, Walmajarri people remain in Fitzroy Crossing as displaced persons on other people's land. For this reason, if for no other, they cling to the memory of their country in the sandhills. There are other reasons, of course: reasons of tradition, of sentiment, of culture.

Living outside their country was one thing for Ngarta and Jukuna's generation, whose identity as desert people was assured. But for their children and grandchildren, as for those of other desert peoples, there was no such certainty. They grew up knowing they were Walmajarri but without knowing Walmajarri country. They did not learn about the sandy desert that had nurtured the countless generations of their ancestors, but about the savanna grasslands to which they did not truly belong. Most were taught hunting by their parents, but the river became the focus of their outdoor lives. Though the older people maintained some ritual life, much of it had been linked to specific events and places in the desert and they no longer had opportunities to perform many of their former ceremonies.

This brief summary of the changes to which the desert people were exposed does not take account of the even more pervasive effects of European culture. White people imposed their language, education, religion, economy and control on all who came within their ambit. The first generation of Walmajarri settlers, as they grew older, saw their children and their grandchildren growing up in a world very different from their own.

Until the mid-1980s there had been no way for most desert people to get back to their homelands. It was no longer practicable to go on foot. Not only had people lost the habit of walking for hundreds of miles, but no one was now living in the sandhills or awaiting their return. The society that had thrived there just a few decades before had vanished. Over the thirty or forty years since they had left, people had adapted to the money economy, though they remained on its bottom rung; their children attended schools and were growing up in a different culture, and to think about returning to their former life as full-time hunters and gatherers was not realistic. Nevertheless, ties to country remained powerful. Walmajarri people belonged and continue to belong to Walmajarri country as to nowhere else on Earth.

A few desert people made visits back to country during the 1970s. Small groups travelled in the company of anthropologists, on whom they were dependent for four-wheel-drive transport, and mining companies occasionally flew a senior person over the sandhills to check that proposed explorations would not encroach on significant sites. However, during the mid-1980s Walmajarri and other desert people started to go back to country in large numbers. Several circumstances made this possible; first among these was the activity of the mining and exploration companies during the seventies and eighties, which had driven seismic lines, as wide as roads and straight as spears, deep into the arid lands formerly almost unexplored by white people. Then there was the growing freedom of Aboriginal people to make their own decisions. Although people were turned off stations in the 1970s and few found other employment, they received unemployment benefits or pensions and some families pooled their money and started to own cars. Concurrently with these developments, and partly as a result of them, the outstation movement was in full swing; since the early 1970s extended families from various language groups had been moving away from their adoptive towns and settlements and setting up small encampments, known as outstations, on or close to their own country.

In 1983, Ngarta and her sister Jukuna, with their husbands Munangu (Hughie) and Pijaji (more commonly known by his nickname, Kurrapakuta), made their first journey south along the seismic lines to see where they led and to select a site for an outstation they wanted to set up for their families. On that occasion they were accompanied by social workers and by linguists Eirlys Richards and Joyce Hudson, who were keen to assist and see the country they had heard so much about. Later, they pooled funds and bought their own four-wheel-drive vehicle. With minimal financial help, they occupied a site near a bore left by a mining company, attached a hand pump to the bore, and erected a couple of bough shades and a canvas shelter. Over the next few months they took out some metal bed frames and a few cooking pots, and set up camp. The outstation, which later moved to a site with better water several kilometres away, was named Kurlku. Although Kurlku was on the edge of the desert, just beyond the most southerly pastoral lease and a long way north of Jukuna and Ngarta's home country, it was Walmajarri land, and the families stayed there with the blessing of the old Walmajarri people who were the local traditional owners.

From their base at Kurlku the exiles were for the first time able to travel deeper into the desert, towards their childhood homelands. They did so tentatively at first. They were no longer young. They had to test their secondhand vehicles and the directions of the seismic lines. They knew, better than anyone, the dangers of breaking down a long way from water. They also had to familiarise themselves again with country they had not visited since their youth.

Ngarta and Jukuna made many journeys back into the desert with their families, reclaiming the waterholes of their childhood. Following the Mabo decision of 1992, they became active Walmajarri Native Title claimants, and were amongst the many artists who collaborated on the well-known Ngurrara painting, by means of which Walmajarri people presented their claim to the Native Title Tribunal. Both women also exhibited their own work in Australia and overseas. Ngarta died in 2002. Jukuna continued to paint and to write stories in Walmajarri until her own death from kidney failure in 2011.

PAT LOWE

THE WORLD OF THE TWO SISTERS

People who lived in the Great Sandy Desert led a distinctive way of life with their own beliefs and customs. In telling their stories, Jukuna and Ngarta took such aspects of their experience for granted, seldom seeing the need to explain what to them was the obvious. Because Ngarta's story is written in the third person, it has been possible to interweave additional information helpful to readers who don't know the desert or its people. Jukuna, however, told her story in her own words and, while Eirlys Richards has provided a free translation that tries to clarify those things that a word-by-word translation would leave obscure, she has endeavoured to remain faithful to the intention of Jukuna's original. For most readers there will remain a number of questions arising from both stories, not all of which can be answered with certainty.

Desert people did not keep track of their ages in years, but as stages of life. Children were described as newborn, crawling, toddling and so on. As they got older, they demonstrated their growing capabilities by the type of game animals they could catch. All children practised catching small lizards when they were very young, graduating to the more important reptiles such as goannas and pythons, and then to the more difficult mammals, including cats, foxes and dingoes. When talking about the time her relations left her behind in the desert, Ngarta mentions her hunting abilities as a measure of her age: 'They left us when I was a little girl: I couldn't kill anything – pussycat or goanna – I only killed lizards and that mountain devil.' The first time Ngarta killed a cat or a fox was a landmark event.

A girl was considered ready for marriage when her body showed the signs of physical maturation: menstruation along with breast development and pubic hair. She might have been betrothed from birth and presented as a baby to her promised husband, but she did not cohabit with him until she was considered mature enough. A young girl might be sent to her husband's camp before this, to get used to him and to learn her role from an older wife, just as Ngarta first accompanied Jukuna when she got married, but the husband was not allowed to have marital relations with her until the right time. The presence of other wives and the lack of real privacy seem to have ensured that such restrictions were observed. No particular ceremony was associated with the move into one's husband's camp, but the man had a lifelong obligation to provide his parents-in-law with meat and otherwise ensure their wellbeing.

A boy's physical development usually determined his readiness for going through stages of law while, conversely, his progress through the law determined his rank among men, as well as his marriageability.

As with ages, so the passing of time is given much less attention by desert people than by people of European descent. Desert people tell stories that may span many years, and non-Aboriginal people always like to know how long a period elapsed between one episode and another. Since years were not counted, it is seldom possible to know. Eirlys and Pat often put questions of elapsing time to Jukuna and Ngarta. We do know that, when Jukuna left the desert as a young bride her sister had not yet reached puberty, and that by the time Ngarta arrived at Christmas Creek in 1961 she was of marriageable age, and Jukuna already had two children. However, where there are no such milestones, we have often had to accept that some things are unknowable.

Because polygamy was normal practice, maintained by the early marriage of girls and the later marriage of men, children usually grew up with more than one woman in the role of mother. In addition, one's mothers' sisters and half-sisters were, and still are, classified as mothers, while one's father's brothers and half-brothers are also called 'father'. The children of these 'fathers' and 'mothers' are one's 'brothers' and 'sisters'. Besides these close relationships and those that stem from them, including a proliferation of grandparents, uncles, aunties and cousins, the complex 'skin' system places everyone else, close and distant, within the relationship matrix, and is the main determinant of eligibility for marriage. Even non-indigenous people may be allocated to one of the four desert or eight riverside 'skin groups', so that their relationship to all members of a given community can be known and the appropriate behaviours and obligations observed.

A well-known custom among desert and other Aboriginal people is to drop from their vocabulary the names of recently deceased people. To hear such a name is disturbing, reminding the listener of someone who has gone, and therefore other people bearing the same or a similar name will change theirs temporarily, if not for good. This taboo applies not only to personal names, but also to the same or similar words in the general vocabulary. As a result, various words in everyday use are replaced with new ones. The closer the relationship, the longer the taboo on the use of a name is likely to be maintained. This custom is not as inconvenient as it may sound, because proper names are not often used, even in everyday life. Instead, people usually address and speak of one another by relationship terms, a practice that causes much tearing of hair amongst non-indigenous people trying to follow narratives and identify the actors.

In her story, Jukuna tends to omit names, particularly those of deceased relatives, and occasionally these have been supplied to avoid too much confusion, but for the most part we have tried to remain true to her own preferences.

Desert dwellers people their country with a myriad of supernatural beings, some benign, others dangerous or threatening. In the jila, the permanent waterholes or wells, live the kalpurtu or 'snakes', bringers of rain. They are friendly towards familiar visitors but churlish towards strangers and, if angered, are likely to bring destructive storms. In certain hollows in the sandhills, wurruwurru – spirit children – live. They are waiting to enter an embryo in the body of a woman, to be born later as a human child. Their identity is already determined, even before they take on human form. Jukuna tells the story of a spirit brother of hers with a bad attitude, who was held responsible for injuring her grandmother.

In the two stories it soon becomes clear that people's main, though by no means only, occupation was getting food. Although men and women had different roles, men doing more hunting than gathering, and women more gathering than hunting, it is also evident that everyone did some of each. The main weapons people used to kill game were the hunting stick – a carved, tapered length of wood, which could be thrown as well as wielded as a club – and the spear, of which there were several kinds. Women usually carried a digging stick and a hunting stick, but some used certain types of spear as well. The long spear thrown with the aid of a woomera was reserved for men. Children used smaller versions of such weapons. If rocks were at hand, they might serve as missiles to dislodge game from a tree or to stun it. Hunting methods varied only according to the prey animal's habits. Goannas and snakes, as well as burrowing mammals, were usually tracked to their burrow, dug out and killed with a hunting stick. Cats were followed on foot until they went to earth or climbed a tree, at which point a hunting stick was used to finish them off. A kangaroo, fox or dingo was more often killed with a spear. Cats and foxes colonised the desert so long ago that they have become normal prey for desert people.

There are a few apparent discrepancies between the accounts of the two sisters, as might be expected in the retelling of oral narratives many years after the events. One that puzzled the editors at first was the contradiction between the description in Ngarta's story of the woman coated in mud after losing her husband, who so terrified Kurnti, and Jukuna's assertion that widows in the desert did not cover themselves with mud. Jukuna was later able to enlighten us: she confirmed the incident with Kurnti, but said that was the only occasion she knew of when a widow had used mud; in the desert, both men and women coloured their skin with red ochre when mourning a spouse, whereas riverside widows applied mud.

Jukuna's brief recounting of Ngarta's experiences also varies slightly from her sister's account. She is, of course, recalling a story she was told some forty years ago, and it is not surprising if she gets some details wrong. On the other hand, she adds something important missing from her sister's story: how it was that Ngarta's life was spared by the 'two guilty men'.

PAT LOWE

WORKING WITH NGARTA

I first met Ngarta in 1986 in Fitzroy Crossing, where she had been living for many years. Like many Walmajarri people of the Great Sandy Desert, she left her country in the early 1960s to live on cattle stations in the Kimberley. As I got to know Ngarta, she and other members of her family told me bits and pieces about how she came to make that journey. It was an extraordinary story, which I felt should be recorded. Ngarta agreed, and when we got the chance, she and I sat down together while she retold her story more fully. Sometimes I wrote down her words, as accurately as I could, in a notebook. On other occasions I made recordings and transcribed them later. Because the Walmajarri way of telling a story is very different from what I am used to, I asked many questions to fill what I perceived to be gaps in the narrative, so that I could write a chronological sequence of events.

The first version of Ngarta's story, in a translation of Ngarta's own words, was published in *Westerly* magazine in 1991. Friends of mine who read the piece complained that it was too obscure and hard for most English-speaking readers to follow, and advised me to retell it in a freer form, filling in background that Ngarta had not considered necessary to supply. For example, when Ngarta describes her journeys as a child, she names the places she visited without mentioning that they are waterholes, because she takes such knowledge for granted. Similarly, she talks about her own experience as a member of one of the last groups of people to leave the desert, without telling us the reasons for the depopulation of her country.

An important part of the background to Ngarta's story is that of the 'two guilty men', who played such a momentous role in her early life, and that of her family. I pieced this together over time from information given to me by a number of people. The different versions do not coincide in every detail, as retold tales seldom do, but they agree in all essentials, and an account is provided as a prologue to Ngarta's story.

Between 1986 and 1989 I accompanied Ngarta and her relatives on some of their early journeys back to their country. I had the privilege of being with her the first time she revisited Tapu, the main jila for her family. After cutting down and uprooting the wattles now choking the silted-up waterhole, the men set to with a shovel, taking it in turns to dig out the sand. It was hot work and took them several hours.

While the men were digging, the women had scattered and were sitting here and there on the ground nearby, dark heads above the low shrubs. They too were busy, breaking up the ground and collecting jurnta, the small bulbs of a coarse grass that favours salty ground.

Ngarta came up to me and quietly beckoned me to follow her. Underneath a clump of low bushes lay a wide, flat stone. I recognised it as a grinding stone, used by women to grind wattle and grass seed into flour. Ngarta knelt down, lifted one end of the heavy stone and rested it against her lap. The stone had belonged to her grandmother, she told me, caressing the grooves worn deeply into the rock by years of grinding. The stone still showed traces of red ochre, perhaps the last thing Ngarta's grandmother had ground on it.

PAT LOWE

WORKING WITH JUKUNA

I first met Jukuna, a young mother of three, at the Races in Fitzroy Crossing in 1968. My good friend Jirrpangali, her sister-in-law, introduced us. I had been in Fitzroy Crossing for about twelve months, working on the daunting task of learning to speak Walmajarri and documenting it in preparation for Bible translation and literacy work. Jukuna and her family were working on Cherrabun Station and had come in to the Races along with the rest of the workers from the station.

A few years later Jukuna and her family came to live in Fitzroy Crossing. Her husband, Pijaji, came to our men's Walmajarri reading class and learned to read and write the language. When the women's class started, Jukuna was there with her youngest child, who was barely a toddler. By 1980 she was a fluent reader, one of a small number of people who could read and write the language. Walmajarri literature at that time consisted of a collection of booklets of personal experiences, and translations from the Bible. Jukuna mostly liked reading the Bible, which she helped translate. Her skill in writing did not develop as quickly as her reading did, probably because there was little reason for her to write.

By the late 1990s I was no longer living at Fitzroy Crossing, but my work often took me through the town. On one of those occasions, when I was visiting Jukuna at her home in Bayulu, just outside the town, she reached into her bag saying she had written something and wanted to show it to me. To my surprise, she produced a writing pad with three or four pages filled with her Walmajarri writing. 'I have written a story about myself,' she said. 'Will you read it?' I sat there and read an account of a young woman leaving her family in the desert to walk with her husband to the unknown country of the white people. I wondered if this might be the first autobiography written by a Walmajarri person in her language.

Some time later the Kimberley Language Resource Centre offered its support for Jukuna to expand the story for possible publication. She was enthusiastic and I was employed to work with her. Our sessions together produced a wealth of information about the desert and the life Jukuna lived there, then the reunion with relations and discovery of many new things as she entered the river country. *Wangki Ngajukura Jiljingajangka* is the result. At her request, I translated the story into English. Pat Lowe, with input from Jukuna and me, edited the English to bring it to its present form.

EIRLYS RICHARDS

WALMAJARRI PRONUNCIATION GUIDE

Some Walmajarri terms used in *Two Sisters* have no exact English equivalents and have been left untranslated in the English texts. Japingka and Japirnka are alternative pronunciations of the name of a particular waterhole.

Walmajarri has 23 different sounds, some of which are not found in English.

VOWELS

a	like the *a* in about and the *u* in cup, e.g. yakapiri (green birdflower bush).
aa	like the *a* in path, e.g. kaajuwal (camel).
i	like the *i* in kid, e.g. jila (underground spring).
ii	like the *ee* in meet, e.g. tiimarnana (aching).
u	like the *u* in put and the *oo* in book, e.g. jumu (soak).
uu	like the *oo* in choose, e.g. muupinya (looked for).

CONSONANTS

j	like the *j* in jump and the *dg* in bludger, e.g. jilji (sandhill).
k	like the *k* in skip and the *gg* in lugger, e.g. kartiya (white person) luka (mud).
l	like the *l* in lick, e.g. lamparn (small).
ly	has no English equivalent. It is similar to the *lli* sound in stallion but not like the *ly* in only, e.g. walyarra (river sand), walypa (wind).

m	like *m* in mud, e.g. mayaru (building).
n	like *n* in nest, e.g. naji (cave).
ng	like the *ng* in singer and long, e.g. manga (girl). It comes at the beginning of many Walmajarri words, for example: ngapa (water).
ny	has no English equivalent. It is similar to the *ni* sound in onion but not like the *ny* in many, e.g. nyanarti (that), parnany (old woman), manyan (sleep).
p	like the *p* in spit and the *b* in sober, e.g. parri (boy), yapa (child).
r	like the *r* in rock and worry, e.g. makura (large coolamon).
rl	like the *rl* in Carl (where the r is sounded, as in American English), e.g. turlurlu (traditional boys' game).
rn	like the *rn* in darn (where the r is sounded, as in American English), e.g. maparn (medicine man).
rr	like the Scottish rolled *r*, e.g. kunyarr (dog); in the middle of a word may sound like a soft d), e.g. parri (boy).
rt	like the *rt* in smart and bird (where the r is sounded, as in American English), e.g. kalpurtu (water serpent).
t	like the *t* in stop and the *dd* in ladder, e.g. Tingarri (an important ceremony), pitipiti (girls' traditional game).
w	like the *w* in wash, e.g. yawarta (horse).
y	like the *y* in yes, e.g. yani (went).

Note: In Walmajarri, the first syllable of the word is normally stressed.

GLOSSARY

age-mates two or more people born around the same time.

antbed a colloquial term for termite mound.

bore cattle station bore for watering cattle, with associated windmill and troughs; by extension, an outstation camp for people who tended the bore, and their families.

coolamon elongated wooden dish made from certain types of tree; people made coolamons of various sizes and shapes to serve different purposes; the term has been adopted into English.

cousin-brother father's brother's son; mother's sister's son. This term is a concession to mainstream terminology: amongst Kimberley and desert language-groups, a cousin-brother or cousin-sister is considered and referred to as a brother or sister.

cry to keen; people cry together following a bereavement, or when they have been separated for a long time.

hairstring length of cord spun from human or animal hair and used for headbands and hairbelts, or for tying or binding.

jaminyjarti fasting by a bereaved person. People who have lost a close relative abstain from eating certain types of meat.

jarriny conception totem. When a woman becomes pregnant, she and/or her husband has a dream that reveals both her pregnancy and the spiritual origin, or jarriny, of the coming child. The jarriny might be an animal, a plant or a feature of the land.

jila
permanent underground waterhole or well, without which human life in the desert would have been impossible. During the dry weather, as the ephemeral waterholes and jumu dried up progressively, people congregated around the jila. Jila had to be dug out afresh when people returned after an absence.

jilji
sandhill; seif dune; these dunes run in parallel lines, sometimes for many kilometres.

jumu
soak; temporary source of undergound water.

jurnta
bulb of a grass (*Cyperus bulbosus*); also known as bush onion.

kalpurtu
water serpent or 'snake'; a spirit being that inhabits certain jila. It has a personality, and may be dangerous or quiet. Dangerous kalpurtu, if angered, can cause high winds and storms.

kana
digging stick; implement used mainly by women for probing animal burrows and digging for root vegetables.

kartiya
'white' person/non-Aboriginal person; a term widely used in the Kimberley and parts of the Northern Territory.

law
ceremonial life; male or female secret/sacred business; young men undergoing their period of initiation are said to be 'going through law'.

marnta
edible gum of the turtujarti tree (*Owenia reticulata*).

ngamaji
mother; mother's sister.

ngarlka
nut of the turtujarti tree (*Owenia reticulata*).

ngarrangkarni creation time, usually known in English as the dreamtime. During this period, the landscape features and life forms were created and named by heroic beings.

puluru edible grass seeds.

puturu type of edible grass seed.

rations station workers used to be paid in rations, which usually consisted of tea, sugar, flour, clothes, blankets and tobacco.

sing to sing someone is to heal or to harm a person, or attract a lover, through a powerful song.

woomera spear-thrower; the term has been adopted into English.

wurruwurru spirit child; these spirits live in certain places, waiting to be born as children.

yakapiri green bird-flower bush, (*Crotalaria cunninghamii*); sandals are made from strips of the bark.

yirnti thin stick, usually broken from a dead wattle tree, used to probe animal burrows and to move food around the fire during cooking.

ACKNOWLEDGEMENTS

The authors are grateful to the following people who contributed in their different ways to making this book: Kim Akerman, Karen Dayman, Joyce Hudson, Nyangarni, the late Jimmy Pike, Fiona Skyring and the late Winingali.

Thanks to Belinda Cook and the Mangkaja Arts Centre for providing the images of the artworks from their archives.

Thank you to the team at Magabala Books, particularly our two editors, Rachel Bin Salleh and Rachael Christensen, for their dedication to this project.

ABOUT THE AUTHORS

Ngarta Jinny Bent spent her early years in the Great Sandy Desert. After her courageous escape from peril in her early teens, she arrived at Christmas Creek Station in 1961. Ngarta was put to work but before long, with the aid of her family, she ran away to Cherrabun Station to join the man who had been chosen as her husband, and later raised a family. In middle age she learned to paint, and her work has been exhibited in Australia and overseas. In her later years Ngarta spent much of her time on her family's outstation, Kurlku, on the edge of the desert, from where she made many journeys back to her country. She died in 2002.

Jukuna Mona Chuguna was a young woman when she walked out of the desert with her husband and members of his family. They worked on cattle stations, then in the early 1970s moved to the Mission at Fitzroy Crossing. Jukuna was among the first women to attend Walmajarri literacy classes. She was a keen student and began working with linguists editing and translating. When the Education Department implemented Indigenous language programmes, Jukuna taught Walmajarri at the Fitzroy Crossing School. She later studied at the Karrayili Adult Education Centre where she began painting the waterholes of her homeland. Jukuna travelled widely in Australia and overseas to exhibit her work. She died in 2011.

Pat Lowe was born in the United Kingdom and taught English in France and East Africa before studying psychology at Liverpool University. She migrated to Western Australia in 1972 and worked as a psychologist in Community Welfare and WA Prisons. In 1986 Pat joined Walmajarri artist Jimmy Pike at his camp in the desert and later moved with him to Broome. She collaborated with him on several books. It was through Jimmy that Pat met his nieces, Ngarta and Jukuna, and shared some of their desert journeys. Pat has published widely.

Eirlys Richards was born in Collie, Western Australia, and began her working life as a primary school teacher. In the late 1960s she moved to Fitzroy Crossing and began studying Walmajarri, a desert language, with the goal of promoting literacy and translating the Bible into Walmajarri. Now living in Broome, Eirlys maintains her link with Walmajarri people through language projects and her friendships. She has produced and contributed to a number of publications about the Walmajarri language, culture and ecological knowledge, and is the go-to person for Walmajarri translation into English.

Aboriginal and Torres Strait people are advised that this publication contains names and images of deceased persons. Approval has been obtained from the appropriate people to publish these names and images.

First published Magabala Books 2016. New edition 2019. Reprinted 2020, 2021
(Shout out to our mates who first published this at Fremantle Arts Centre Press, 2004)
Magabala Books Aboriginal Corporation, Broome, Western Australia
Website: www.magabala.com Email: sales@magabala.com

Magabala Books receives financial assistance from the Commonwealth Government through the Australia Council, its arts advisory body. The State of Western Australia has made an investment in this project through the Department of Local Government, Sport and Cultural Industries. Magabala Books would like to acknowledge the support of the Shire of Broome, Western Australia.

Two Sisters has been published with the support of private donors through the Magabala Books Literary Fund, including the J & C Stewart Family Foundation, the Spinifex Trust and Australian Creative Partnerships through Plus1. You all rock.

Magabala Books is Australia's only independent Aboriginal and Torres Strait Islander publishing house. Magabala Books acknowledges the Traditional Owners of the Country on which we live and work. We recognise the unbroken connection to traditional lands, waters and cultures. Through what we publish, we honour all our Elders, peoples and stories, past, present and future.

Cover and artwork Jo Hunt
Typeset by the very talented Jo Hunt
Printed by Ovato Print Pty Ltd

The facsimile of Jukuna's handwriting featured on the inside cover has been taken from a page of the original writing of her story. Article on p43 reproduced with permission, West Australian Newspapers.

9781925936780 (paperback)

 A catalogue record for this book is available from the National Library of Australia

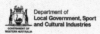